Far From the Tree

A Memoir

By
Pat Higgins Adelhardt

So Karen —
So glad we've met
Pat Higgins Adelhardt

This is a work of creative nonfiction. Conversations in the book are the author's recollections and imaginings with the intention of capturing the essence of the dialogues presented, not word-for-word transcripts.

10 Digit ISBN: 0-578-53008-2
13 Digit ISBN: 978-0-578-53008-6

FIRST EDITION
Inlet Shade Publishing 2019

Contact: adelhardtpat@gmail.com

Cover art design by David Jennings
Rear cover portrait by Robin Sommer, MidAtlantic Photographic LLC
Wallowa Lake photo by the author

DEDICATED TO

Brian, my loving husband,

son Bryce, grandson Mason,

and to my siblings: Ellen, Maureen, and Pete.

I am optimistic that you will take into account that herein

is my memory and recollections

and they will probably differ from your own.

Far From the Tree

The apple doesn't fall far from the tree,
   or so they say.

But what about the ones whisked away
   by a soaring spirit?

Perhaps a few were meant to fly.

D.A. Jennings

Table of Contents

Reptile Release 1

Wouldn't You Like to Know? 5

Cracked Foundation.. 7

Oregon or Bust 10

Death in the City.. 23

Faith and Fiction 32

Pecking Order 36

Odell, Oregon... 40

School Days... 44

Freshman Shadows.. 57

The Twist and Truth... 64

Travel Is Broadening 67

Pitchfork 84

Go East Young Woman, Go East........................... 89

Undaunted.. 101

Turn Around Joe 113

Tested 149

These Little Piggies Go to Market 163

Frayed Edges 167

Moving On 175

Small Package 184

Child-Rearing 192

Downward Spiral 194

Agri-Tourism 199

It's Only Money 207

Road Trip 211

A Piece of Oregon 218

Hidden Treasure 224

Letting Go 226

Acknowledgements 233

Reptile Release

Temperatures rose to the nineties and clammy humidity tagged along. Sweat trickled down my sides as I sat on an upturned apple crate in our log barn, built in the 1700's, as I priced and processed orders of stuffed farm animals and toy tractors for display in the barn gift shop. In partnership with the bank, my husband Brian and I purchased this farm sixteen years earlier in 1975. We christened it Applewood Farm in deference to the five very old apple trees that grew beyond the chestnut log house and with a nod to my upbringing on an apple-and-pear orchard in the great Northwest. Our 100-acre farm was located mostly on the Maryland side of the Mason Dixon Line—the border between Pennsylvania and Maryland. Local lore claimed the old farmhouse had served as a stagecoach rest stop for travelers between Philadelphia and Washington, D.C., and as an underground railway safe shelter for slaves escaping to the north. Time swallowed most of the historical details of the old farm, but without doubt the rich soil nourished rotating crops as well as the weeds.

Our agricultural practices evolved from traditional crop farming of corn and soybeans to growing acres of Christmas trees for retail sale. Customers came to "choose and cut" their trees in December. We added new attractions like pony rides, horse drawn carriage rides, hayrides and the gift shop to keep customers interested in returning.

About eight years earlier we cleaned the old log barn of its moldy straw and critters and it became our center of operations. The gift shop was my responsibility and involved a year long process of ordering, unpacking, pricing, decorating and organizing attractive displays.

These repetitive tasks absorbed the hours and brought on long shadows as the sun began its western descent. Hot and sweaty, I headed toward the house to figure out what to have for dinner. Since Brian was off at his sailing job captaining a

Chesapeake Bay oyster dredging boat, I was cooking for Bryce, our preteen son, and me. Bryce's mini four-wheeler rumbled as he rolled up. "Hey, Mom what's for dinner?" he hollered through the open sliding glass doors.

"Just got in from the barn, what do you feel like?" I replied.

"Can we have tacos?"

"Sure, be back and ready to eat at 6 o'clock, okay?"

Bryce and I sat down at the round dining table just inside the glass doors that opened to the screened front porch. Out of the corner of my eye I saw movement to my right. Bryce jumped to his feet, shouting, "Mom! Mom! I think I just saw a sa—aaa—nnnake!"

"What? Where?" I gasped.

"It slithered under the table. I think it's a black snake...and long!" Bryce shouted. With a screech I jumped up, crashing into the sliding glass door. The clear panes reverberated but held. I almost knocked myself out in my panic. Sure enough the evil thing rested nearby wrapped around the dining table pedestal.

"Run to the barn and get a pitchfork. We've got to get him out of here," I said. As Bryce ran toward the barn, I tried to make a plan, but my mind could only absorb the image of this dark impending danger. It seemed to represent everything going on in my life at the moment. Recently diagnosed with depression, I felt like a shell of my former self. I'd realized, with Brian's encouragement and the recommendation of my OBGYN doctor, some professional help was in order to help me sort through issues bubbling beneath the surface. When I looked for the Pat I knew, she'd stepped out. How long would it last? What caused it? Why did I look normal to everyone when I felt far from it? Sleep disrupted, food tasteless, thoughts scattered, decisions non-existent, creativity in the toilet. Living on a farm, I saw farmhands harvest and hoist hay bales easily, but here I was, unable to balance what felt like a fifty-pound cloud overhead. The cloud wavered from gray to black as days wore on. I was accustomed to facing life's dragons and slaying them on my own, but this depression was elusive. Stubborn as that damned black snake.

A broom handle served as my prod. As I jabbed, the snake's pink-forked tongue licked the air. He curled tighter around the table pedestal mirroring my grip on my dark cloud as I tried to hold on to things. With each poke the snake lashed out. He was comfortable where he was and wanted me to leave him alone. I looked into his beady eyes and I could relate. For weeks, my psychiatrist Rita had been pushing me to explore the depths of my subconscious and unearth family secrets that had accumulated over a long time. They were tucked away, deep inside, to hide and percolate with each advancing year.

Bryce, returning with the weapon of destruction, said, "Mom he's starting to move a little. When he unwinds, I'll try to head him across the porch and through the door, just watch yourself as I nudge him along."

Slowly, our scaly visitor gave up his stranglehold, loosening his ebony length. He seemed to recognize that the tall green grass of his natural habitat would be friendlier than an annoying kid with a five-tined pitchfork. After a spell that stretched with many stops and starts, Bryce successfully cajoled the snake across the porch and out the screen door. Scooping up the snake on the fork tines as it writhed and hissed, Bryce rushed the snake toward the pasture fence and hurled him to freedom.

Like our slithery visitor, I experienced many starts and stops along the way to recovery. The realization that I was almost comfortable with the fear as my constant companion and had not wanted to release it. Each session with Rita eased the coils of anxiety hidden in my subconscious. She helped me recognize that it was time to quit tamping down and ignoring the things that set my teeth on edge: my mother-in-law's shoddy treatment of me, Brian's devil-may-care approach to money, my mother's misplaced anger and resentment towards me.

My freedom would not come so quickly or so easily. Fifty-plus years pressed down on me. Born into a family already

3

cloaked under layers of secrecy far beyond my young comprehension we migrated from east to west. Like the snake in the house, the untangling came, but it would not be without pain.

Wouldn't You Like to Know?

My father, Joe Higgins, brought our family to Odell, Oregon in 1945 to make his mark on the world. He left behind the lights, crowds, corruption, and his mother and 12 siblings in New York City. He adapted quickly to this tiny town sequestered and encircled by the Cascade Mountains on the outskirts of Hood River.

A crop of wavy, tar-colored hair topped off his tan skin and short stature. Dad knew little of how to care for the cherries in his newly acquired orchard, and so he traveled the valley asking questions of successful orchardists with an eye on one day acquiring acreage with apple and pear trees. A conversation with this brash and amusing man proved interesting and entertaining to the locals and he easily won them over. Part of his charm rested in the fact that he wasn't afraid to admit his lack of knowledge about horticultural practices and he recognized and sought out the expertise and proven practices of other orchardists.

When the Second World War ended, many Japanese returned to the valley from internment camps hoping to reclaim the orchards they had been forced to leave. Instead, they faced opposition and discrimination from many of the Caucasians in the valley. However, Dad identified with these displaced Japanese, more than many of the people who looked like him, because they shared a love of fostering life, of dirt and hard work to build an orchard to support a family and their techniques produced beautiful fruit.

Dad set about helping the Japanese families reacclimate. In return, Joe learned a whole new approach to growing things as the Japanese orchardists shared their horticultural expertise. Over the years this symbiosis proved beneficial to all, and Dad's orchard thrived, as did his standing in the community.

Dad conveyed a mysterious air that contradicted his colorful and entertaining side. The green aviator glasses he wore to hide his expressive gold-flecked hazel eyes contributed to the allure. "Your eyes are the windows to your soul," he asserted often, insisting it important to keep the eyes guarded against folks reading one's innermost thoughts. His musings were also protected by sarcastic humor, which discouraged all but the hardiest people willing to scale that pointed fence and count themselves in the small circle of Dad's friends. This entitlement however, still did not make them privy to his most guarded secrets.

Joe Higgins possessed the physical attributes of an Irishman coupled with his Irish surname. In fact, he was born to an Italian father and Irish mother but claimed only Irish heritage upon our relocation to Oregon. My mother, two sisters, brother and I lived our days tensely trying to rise to my father's many expectations and edicts. Like jugglers, we struggled to keep all the balls airborne, knowing that his scathing ridicule would be the consequence of a slipup. I understood early on that what happened in our curtained home was not to be divulged or aired in public under any circumstance. When asked by a new acquaintance why he'd come all the way from New York City to settle in the west, Dad quipped, with a quirky smile, "Wouldn't you like to know?" Then he smoothly changed the subject.

Dad was tough, stern, hardworking, generous, humorous, and deceptive. Mom was gentle, explosive, creative, fun, vulnerable, tireless, organized and funny. I grew up uneasily under my parents' tutelage. The struggle to maintain a balance through what I learned from each of them pushed and pulled me. There was no escaping that explosive formula.

6

Cracked Foundation

Dad and Mom married in 1939. She was 11 years younger and immeasurably less worldly than Dad's 34 years. They met during the summer at a lake in the Adirondack Mountains where Mom and her sister Charlotte vacationed with a group of girlfriends. In pictures from that time, Mom and Dad made a striking couple. He was handsome, a little taller than she, with dark wavy hair and hazel eyes. She was slender, classy, and beautiful with compelling crystal blue eyes. Dad was born into a large, Italian-Irish family of thirteen children, wrought with tension, silence, and hostility while Mom's resonated with warmth and closeness. Mom was German by birth, raised in a small family with only one sister.

Dad worked as a wholesale fruit broker on the docks of New York City. He sold fresh fruit to shop owners who came daily, prior to opening their stalls and stores. Employed by Recordac Machines, Mom was organized and an excellent typist. On meeting Mom, Dad introduced himself as Joe Higgins. Mom discovered only after Dad placed a perfect, 2-1/2 caret marquis diamond on her finger that Dad had recently changed his name from Loschiavo to his mother's maiden name, Higgins—an attempt to jettison his Loschiavo Sicilian-Italian heritage forever. He swore Mom to secrecy, starting a pattern of concealment that threaded its way through their entire married life. I can imagine Mom feeling anxious about meeting her new in-laws and all those siblings for the first time. Dad's recent name change was like the elephant in the room. The Loschiavo family knew about this radical action and were not pleased or sympathetic to Dad's rationale for it.

On the social and economic ladder in 1930s New York City, the Irish stood one rung up—less discriminated against than the Italians. I also suspect that the Italian Mafia, a looming presence in the daily lives of those living and working in Brooklyn, played a role in Dad's decision to go west. Those Italian mobsters had a hand in most commerce on the docks, and I imagine Dad wanted to distance himself from their influence, though he never admitted this to me outright.

Frank Costello ascended to the throne of Mafia Boss in 1936. Costello loved the role, calling his Capos to his suite at the New York Plaza Hotel. These high-ranking Mafia men passed on his orders to their "soldiers" who traversed across New York to conquer the city in his name. He ruled the unions that controlled the piers and docks of New York and New Jersey. In effect, this made Costello the governor over movement of virtually all freight in and out of America. His family owned the garment industry, the construction business, trash collection, the catering industry, restaurants, bars, nightclubs, and theaters. He placed a tax on almost everything sold or traded, raking in millions of dollars. Escaping Mafia control if you made your living in a small wholesale fruit business on the docks, as did Dad, would have been virtually impossible.

Dad rose every morning at two and took the train from the stylish, well-manicured Manhasset, Long Island, home where I, as a wee three year old, slept peacefully along with my Mom and two sisters, Ellen and Maureen. He arrived at the docks by four to begin his day. One-stop grocery stores such as A&P and Safeway were in their infancy at this time and Dad could see his way of doing business was waning. When he married Mom, Dad was not on speaking terms with his father, with whom he worked on the docks. Perhaps his father cooperated with the Mafia, which caused the falling out between them. Regardless, the environment grew increasingly challenging; it was time to consider other options.

An invitation came from Roy Webster, one of Dad's fruit suppliers, a prominent orchardist and Bishop of the Mormon Church in Hood River, Oregon. Roy asked Dad to travel across the country with him to see this lush valley where mostly cherries, apples and pears were grown. The trip was the spark that ignited the Higgins family's relocation to the Great Northwest and changed everything. While in the west, Dad purchased a small cherry orchard with a nice home on Orchard Road quiet, with a lovely view of Mt Hood. Returning home, he announced to us that we were moving west that summer.

Leaving what she knew and loved must have felt terrifying to mom, and yet it was an exciting challenge, like jumping from a plane for the first time. She knew no one and only had stories of cowboys and Indians to guide her. Each mile put her farther and farther from that busy city-world with its bright lights, glamour, excitement, and real dangers, too. Landscapes changed from skyscrapers, traffic congestion and people rushing about to barns and rustic dwellings, gently rolling fields of crops and then the flat Midwest as it spread endlessly before us.

I wonder if Mom could have guessed at that time the effect my father's moods and bleak silences—a decided counterpoint to her caring tenderness—would have on our family household. Departing New York surely meant leaving behind secrets on both sides that would only be disclosed with time. Dad was taking us to the other side of the continent, a distance of 3500 miles where we knew no one except for Dad's fruit-business associate. Naïve easterners, we pictured mail delivery by pony express riders, galloping from outpost to outpost just like in the wild and wooly western movies popular at that time.

Oregon or Bust

The Higgins family of five migrated from New York in 1945. I was three-and-a-half years old. We drove across the country in our green two-door Plymouth, three squirmy girls in the back seat, Mom and Dad in the front. We relieved the monotony of the road by playing games. "Pick the car color" was an easy favorite. Blue was my chosen color, and Mom, Dad, Ellen and Maureen each selected their favorites. Each of us counted the number of passing cars that matched our chosen color on the narrow, two-lane Interstate 30. When we tired of counting we counted up colors to see who won.

Along the way billboards, mile after mile, claimed that a place outside a small Midwestern town had a two-headed calf. We stopped, excited for a break in the drive. Dad pulled into the driveway of an isolated farmhouse not far off the main road. As we entered the small, shadowed living room we saw the strange calf—not real, but stuffed, positioned on the fireplace hearth. I felt strange and my stomach went jittery as I reached for Mom's hand. Animal oddities were popular at carnivals in the forties and were called "freak shows." Medical advances and public opinion changed over the years, and the shows diminished, rarely seen now. I can still hear my parents laughing as we traveled on after viewing the unusual sight. I didn't get the humor. For years after, the mention of this incident sent my parents into gales of warm laughter, induced, no doubt, by the memory of the tedium of the road, trapped in the car for hours with three fidgety girls.

I also remember seeing Old Faithful erupt hundreds of feet in the air at Yellowstone National Park, like a giant roaring for purchase, filling me with awe. Cool, moist, rainbow mist fell on my upturned, freckled face. All around, I saw majestic mountains, massive evergreens—such contrast to the leafy, deciduous trees of the East. I remember Mom turning her face upward as well, closing her eyes, capturing the moment, and now I understand that she must have felt as amazed as I did. She often repositioned the furniture and rugs in our living room if she felt trapped in one place for too long. Meeting new people and experiencing new things was a passion of hers, and the grandeur and mystery of Yellowstone would not have been lost on her.

Despite Dad's stern demeanor, my memories of this trip and early days in Hood River are filled with light, like rays of sunshine piercing a gloomy day. Because I was only three-and-a-half years old, specifics elude me of that time, but my sense is that Dad was in good humor, having extricated his family from the East. He was on his way to realizing his dream.

We arrived at our new home on Orchard Road in early summer and began exploring. The two-story house was big and comfortable with white clapboard on the outside and large, green-shuttered windows facing Mt. Hood to the south. A one-car garage stood behind the house, its opening dark and shadowy. Its window at the peak of the roof would be the future scene of an attempted flight—though my vigilant mother would abort the simulation and save my friend and me from the certainty of broken bones. Next to the garage stood a sizeable fenced turkey coop and a picker's shack to house itinerate help during harvest.

A few deciduous trees were outnumbered by large, stately evergreens standing like sentinels. The perimeter of the yard was both hedged and fenced with lots of grass for tumbling, running, and games of tag. An impressive glassed-in sunroom framed the south side of the house, off the large living room. This treasured sanctuary became the family playroom. Many drizzly, gray, cold fall and winter days and nights were spent in this sunroom. We drew, painted, played cards and board games, danced, and read.

Outside laid a manicured English style garden with cobbled walks, benches, and arches. In fair weather, this room was as an enchanting place to concoct games of "daring do," hide and seek, or playing wedding bride. Ellen, Maureen and I often glided demurely down the cobbled steps, a net veil floating in the lucky girl's wake, and singing, "Here Comes the Bride."

The cherry orchard, while not large, held green, leafy, climb-able trees with rough-smooth bark that bore more cherries than could be eaten. The cherries were bright red—sweet, stain-your-mouth-and-dribble-down-your-chin juicy with tiny pits and perfect for spitting.

Directly across the quiet road in an enchanting gray Victorian house, lived Mrs. Rodwell, a cultured and educated woman. Mrs. Rodwell welcomed us on our arrival and became a trusted family friend. We girls called her "Roddie" but never to her face. A disrespectful display of that magnitude would be cause for a verbal reprimand in our household.

Spending time with Mrs. Rodwell was always memorable. Often I'd stop in to visit and I remember I arrived early one morning. We chatted while she fixed her face and hair in a small bathroom off the kitchen.

"Pat, let me show you how to make a rat's tail," she said.

"A rat's tail! What is that?" My reflection in the mirror looked anxious.

"I'm going to show you. First I comb my hair and get all the snarls out of it, like this." She combed the long strands of her graying red hair with fluid, sweeping strokes. "Then I take the hair from my brush and roll it between the palms of my hands into a long coil. It takes quite a bit of hair to make it just right...see, here is one I have been working on."

"It doesn't look like a rat, Mrs. Rodwell."

"Well, we just call it that because it is long and thin like a big rat's tail," she chuckled.

"Why do you do it?" I asked.

"I use these to put under my own hair to make it puffy and full and most of all pretty. Here, want to feel?" Soft and sort of cushy, the tail seemed strange to my young senses. Wadded in red and gray, the strands seemed more like a rat's nest than a tail.

After she finished her morning ritual, we returned to Roddie's windowed kitchen. The sun filtered softly as she set up a large, flute-edged copper pan at a small wooden table where we placed her china closet treasures. I selected all manner of glass animals and objects: frogs, birds, snails, reptiles, fish, bears, deer, horses, cows, shells and many multi-colored marbles. She had collected these in her world travels and they were surely delicate and expensive. No matter! I was permitted to arrange these treasures in the large fluted pan. Roddie added water and my imagination ran, entertained for joyous hours. The water shimmered, reflecting the colors of my lovely, enchanting play-friends.

As I played, Roddie regaled me with tales of her life as a young, married missionary in the Far East. All the while, she worked at her daily chores. She puttered at the kitchen sink or baked something delectable that caused cinnamon smells to waft throughout the kitchen. With Roddie as my neighbor, I never pined for friends my own age. Playtime back East revolved around my Mom and two older sisters, who most times found me in the way or a nuisance. Now I had someone who seemed to genuinely appreciate me, and I her.

I imagine Mom also enjoyed a kinship with Mrs. Rodwell, finding in her someone who knew and understood the finer things in life. Occasionally, I shared Roddie with my sisters. She would assemble us in her sunny living room for an afternoon lesson in Contract Bridge. Imagine the patience of the woman who taught a four, six, and eight-year-old to play this complex game.

One afternoon when I came for a visit, instead of bustling about as usual, I could see Roddie lying on the beige living room sofa. I tiptoed in from the kitchen, through the dining room, and up to the sofa. I saw her eyes were closed.

"Who's there?" she said.

"It's me, Mrs. Rodwell. What's the matter? Are you okay?" I placed my small hand on her wrinkled forehead, as my mother did to me when I was sick. Mom was sympathetic and compassionate when we were sick or threatened with Dad's "strap."

13

"I just felt very tired and a little sick to my stomach. I'll be fine. You are kind, my little friend, to care."

"Should I go and get my Mom?" She would know what to do. An anxious knot grew in my tummy. I knew we did not live close to a hospital and had no idea about doctors, how to get them or what to do if someone became ill.

"No, Pat, that's okay. I'll be fine after a little rest. Would you sit next to the sofa and keep me company for a spell? I'll be fit as a fiddle in a bit." And soon, she was. Our days continued, filled with new discoveries.

Other neighbors who lived up the road a piece were the Jensens who had kids more our age. Their huge red bull always lay in their front yard chewing its cud under a massive spreading maple tree. The bull was a scary creature with a chain extending from the ring in his nose to the trunk of the tree where it was wrapped, I hoped securely. I trusted the sturdy tree would hold him. Having circumvented the bull many times, we Higgins girls spent hours frolicking in the straw and hayloft of the big red barn with the Jensen kids. I remember a long rope in the hayloft with a knot on the end. We grabbed hold of the rope, and swung out over the piles of new hay below and with a screech tumbled into that sweet, pungent pillow of green.

At day's end I liked to walk down the dirt lane beside our property. There I'd find the neighbor's dark brown mule and a small gray donkey munching hay in their stalls. Both had luminous, expressive brown eyes. I imagined they could tell captivating tales if they could do more than *braaaay* at the top of their lungs. They must have been the spark kindling my interest in mules and burros that resurfaced much later in my life.

Dad and Mom decided to raise turkeys since they had a ready-made turkey coop. I imagine Dad thought Thanksgiving would bring a nice profit. Ellen, Maureen and I helped feed and water the turkeys. None of us liked entering the smelly, gooey pen, but it was a chore Dad assigned to us. I cannot remember Dad being present for the turkey roundup. Usually, with the

14

cherry harvest done, he'd take several days and travel to Wenatchee, Washington, attending horticulture meetings with fellow orchardists to learn the latest and best ways to grow the fruit that grew in the Hood River Valley.

The harvesting of the birds fell to Mom, city born and bred. The cornering and capturing of the designated bird involved a great deal of shouting and dashing around the turkey pen: a flurry of wings, pecking and squawks, slipping and sliding *and* all that poop. Eventually, we wrestled the chosen one into the open garage. Mom stretched its writhing neck across the block. With hatchet in hand, her face screwed in distaste, she squeezed her eyes shut...Wham! The unlucky fowl's head flew with a spray of sticky crimson in all directions. Screaming ensued as the body of the bird took on a life of its own, scrambling around the garage.

Once the bird was dead, Mom held it by its feet and plunged it into a large kettle of very hot water, swishing it around as it was scalded. This helped to soften the feathers and eased the picking process. I can still smell that pungent, burning odor. When the bird was picked of all its feathers, Mom stuck her hand inside, removed all the entrails and cleaned the bird in preparation for the customer's Thanksgiving table—a time consuming job. I hope that Mom felt exhilaration, pride and a sense of unique accomplishment once her palm was graced with the rewards of that venture. I suppose my generally positive outlook is the reason for such a wish. Mom's expressive face let me know she hated every minute.

After two years on Orchard Road, Dad bought a 21-acre apple-and-pear-orchard on Davis Road, five miles into the central valley in the small town of Odell. While small, Odell starred as the crossroads for the entire area. Railroad tracks next to the fruit packing plant facilitated the passage of the Mt. Hood Railroad. Rustic boardwalks and hitching posts framed the dirt road. Along the two blocks of Main Street stood a saloon and soda fountain (root beer floats were a family favorite), Eloise and Bish Dunn's Variety Store (with lots of penny candies), the tiny Post Office headed by kind postmistress Mildred Rhoads and LaComb's Grocery, Gerig's gas station book-ended one end of town and Bob Fletcher and Bish Dunn's gas station book-ended the other. Betty Bloom's beauty parlor, Henry's Hardware and the brown-shingled Methodist church completed the lineup. Cherry, apple-and-pear orchards, packing and cold-storage plants, and mills and lumberyards abounded. These were the main industries of the area.

In preparation for our move to Odell, Dad and Mom renovated a dilapidated, weathered structure that was on the new property and was little more than a shack. Dad moved, intact, the large turkey coop from our Orchard Road property and attached it to this sad little building. The coop was designated our living room after we swept it clean and somehow fumigated it. While Mom and Dad worked that summer, we girls spent our days exploring our new surroundings and sipping on root beer floats "around the corner." Mom and Dad applied knotty pine throughout the house: floors, walls and ceilings. Mom's talent and taste for making things look warm and homey, regardless of their outer shell, transformed our home into a welcoming one. Vibrantly colored oriental rugs brought from New York decked the floors, and quality mahogany furniture placed throughout the dining, living room and bedrooms.

The fact that the ceilings were only seven feet high made little difference to a family of half-pints. However, when our friend Roy Webster—who stood six-feet five-inches tall—came to visit, it was a different story. He loved to stand in the middle of our turkey coop-cum-living room and kick the ceiling, making his audience squeal with excitement: "Do it again! Do it again!" As long as I lived in that house and Roy visited, he never failed to perform this feat.

Our pear orchard surrounded the new home in orderly rows and bordered the Davis property to the east. The Davises, also orchardists were one of the more prominent families in Odell. The road we lived on bores their name. They owned a

16

stone-and-cement in-ground swimming pool in their yard, and
Mom deemed their house "very nice." Mom did not like all the
Odell "shacks," her word for houses that didn't meet her East
Coast standards.

I can imagine how she felt, moving again *and* into a place
that didn't measure up. However, Mom liked change and
adventure and the remodel certainly would have provided plenty
of that. Now she would settle into a dwelling she and Dad
designed and built themselves, transforming a shack into a
home—there surely was satisfaction in that accomplishment.

Dad liked to entertain, on his terms. He invited friends and
acquaintances in for a highball or Manhattan, which he whipped
up along with his jokes, stories, and political or financial advice. If
he really felt magnanimous, he would offer a coveted dinner or
dessert, which Mom painstakingly created with much fretting and
anxiety. Even her best efforts would be a source of Dad's ridicule
later.

All her life, Mom questioned her abilities and how she
would be perceived and accepted in the community. This
contradicted the accomplished woman I saw. Dad's demeanor
contributed to her lack of confidence—he undermined any
success she achieved but acted outwardly proud to have her as
his mate. I suspect this behavior made him feel more important
while he worked to conceal his own insecurities.

Situated in the center of the valley, our house often served
as a gathering place for Mom and Dad's friends. Those social
occasions always seemed to result in a fun-filled afternoon or
evening for all, as long as the guests didn't overstay their
welcome. At 8 p.m. sharp, Dad, who until that time would be
happily sitting in his living room chair holding court, would rise
abruptly and without another word toddle off to bed. Mom,
annoyed at his insulting behavior, was left to carry on his social
responsibilities. I learned the flair of gracious entertaining at an
early age, and I also understood through cautionary comments

from Dad and Mom that to reveal underlying family turmoil was socially unacceptable.

Those lighthearted social moments were met in equal measure with more troubling ones. A particularly dark moment in this room, where Dad frequently scolded my siblings and me, is still fresh.

"Butch, didn't I tell you to clean up your toys?" Dad asked sternly. He stood in the doorway between the kitchen and our living room. The black leather, five-tailed strap, nicknamed the "five-tailed monster," dangled menacingly from his right hand, twitching ever so slightly. Dad used this disciplinary tool for offenses he thought particularly grievous. Butch was the nickname Dad had tagged me with as we headed west, as "Pat" was too feminine a name for the role of wished-for son. "Come in here *now* and do it."

At five years old, I looked up at him in terror. What he demanded required me to walk through the narrow doorway crossing in front of him *and* that hated instrument of discipline. I edged forward; twisting sideways hoping that, if Dad lashed out, minimal damage would be inflicted on my skinny legs. That was just it. I could never be sure if the black monster's 5 tails, each 24-inches in length, would cause actual physical pain. Dad let it hover, flicking. Anguish felt like a stone in my gullet. Not one to hedge or dodge a situation, I screwed up my courage and dashed into the toy-strewn living room to collect and store the offending items. I heard Dad's sneering chuckle as I scrambled to set things right. Only then could I escape to the peace and safety of the clean, clear Oregon outdoors that became my haven.

Our house continued to evolve and a similar coop-sized addition became a bedroom for the "girls" and molded the Davis Road home into a "U," with the original shack becoming a new kitchen, dining room, bath, and bedroom. Summer nights were spent right outside the front door, lying on the grass in the protection of the "U". We studied the starry sky, picked out the constellations we learned during summers at Camp Yallani for

Camp Fire Girls, and slept the crisp Oregon nights away in snug sleeping bags.

The remainder of our property included producing fruit trees. At the end of the pear rows stood a large picker's shack and an outhouse tucked into the woods. Down the hill from this shack flowed a sparkling creek. The water's source originated on Mt. Hood, and in it nourished our constant supply of delicious, crisp watercress from spring through fall. A pump house on the creek supplied water to the sprinklers to irrigate the orchard in the summer months. The pump house stood at the end of a long flume that transported the water from the creek. Dad dammed the creek up at the entrance to the woods to divert the water to the pump house.

Every summer the wild mustard, fuzzy cattails, and crisp orchard grass engulfed the flume. Wearing our tall-to-the-knees black orchard boots and with sickles in hand, Ellen, Maureen, and I were tasked with cutting away the weeds obstructing the eight-inch wide boards that lay on top of the flume. The job was hot, sweaty, and buggy and not one of our favorites. It was necessary to walk the plank boards to get the job done because the thick weeds and brush growing beside the flume made it impenetrable. When my turn came to "walk the flume," I tried to balance on the narrow planks as the yellow mustard activated sneezing fits, watery eyes and a runny nose.

Dad paid us $1 per hour and unless he countermanded our wishes, we could spend it as we wanted. He also preached the value of saving. I saved for a whole year when I was eight to buy a bike of my own—used, but a beautiful blue. When Dad refused to let me buy it, I felt my face flush with disappointment, and my stomach clench and I fought, unsuccessfully, to hold back angry tears. It was a bitter pill, being denied my first wheels and a sense of freedom and independence. I don't remember his reasons and likely he didn't offer any, but it reinforced his power and control. This life lesson taught me, at a very impressionable age, that I could save all I wanted and not get what I wanted. Better to spend

19

it as soon as I earned it on candy, Twinkies, and Cream Pies at the corner store. Surely, this lesson was contradictory to whatever Dad thought he conveyed.

Our primary summer orchard chore was changing the irrigation sprinklers twice a day, morning after breakfast and evening before dinner. Lines had to be moved two rows over in the fruit trees. Dad maintained two lines, one in the pears and one in the apples. My sisters changed the sprinklers together, which made the job easier. When I was still quite young and before sprinkler changing was one of my duties, I remember one day they cajoled me into helping.

"Come on, Butch. We'll put you in the middle where it won't be heavy," they said. "You'll have fun."

I went along. My sisters were including me in something! Each pipe was twenty feet long, and with three of us working together we could move two connected pipes at once, weaving 40 feet of pipe between the trees. We skipped the next row and lined up, connecting the pipe in the designated row. It took several years for me to figure out that Ellen and Maureen placed me in the middle because it made it easier on them, leaving me with the hardest and heaviest spot.

Ellen shouted, "Butch would you stop swinging the pipes and hold up the middle!" My sisters made their point by pushing and pulling the pipes back and forth, then sideways. I flailed about, braids flying like a drunken blackbird. The two of them laughed as I stumbled and tripped in oversized orchard boots.

The most hated part of the job came when we changed the sprinklers from one end of the orchard to the other. Inevitably, a sprinkler head broke and needed fixing, or we lost one of the black, bracelet-sized rubber gaskets. When we turned the water on to "check the pipes," it sprayed with abandon but not where it was needed. Dad was not particularly mechanical. We knew we would face grief and demeaning sarcasm, no doubt to mask his frustration over the need to repair something he lacked the skills to attend to.

A new world opened to me beyond where our apple trees grew across the creek via a dirt bridge, just up from the pump house. This orchard block bordered a road we shared with three Fletcher families. Susan Fletcher, my age and a playmate, lived at the end of the lane just beyond an acre of intriguing evergreen woods. Her family owned real milk cows, steers, pigs, and chickens. Our family had only cats and dogs. At Susan's farm I experienced a pig killing. I learned that the cool fall temperatures were ideal for a pig harvest. I didn't witness the actual corralling and killing of the unlucky animal. When I arrived, the huge steaming tank above the smoky wood fire waited for the pig. That colorful vision of the torrents of spurting red blood and the acrid smell of scalding pig flesh as the carcass was lowered into the tank still return vividly to my mind.

Susan had things to fear, like a fox in her family's chicken coop or a steer getting loose, but at least her fears were out in the open, unlike mine. Years later, when I think about my childhood, I wonder about the contrast I felt between my playful exploring and my fearful encounters inside our home.

Every window in our house had Venetian blinds always shut tight, plus drawn curtains to protect against the possible intrusion of nosey neighbors. An undercurrent of tension stoked by Dad kept Mom on edge. She never relaxed or let down her guard, always keeping an ear tuned to Dad's coming and goings. When she heard Dad's imminent arrival, she jumped up and busied herself.

Dad rarely displayed warmth or affection, never complimented or encouraged Mom on a meal despite her exceptional cooking. I don't remember any praise that came my way for work done well either. When I received the coveted Citizenship Award at high school graduation, my best friend's dad cajoled and then embarrassed Dad into uttering a few congratulatory words in my direction. It hurt that it was so hard for him. In our family it was assumed you did your best, and if you fell short you were harshly criticized. We all waited cautiously for the next flare up, never sure what would ignite Dad's ire. Mom called it "walking on egg-shells." If I had words for it at the time, I might have compared our anxiety to droplets of water dancing across a hot skillet.

Death in the City

My legs trembled as I stood in the doorway. The room seemed cavernous and dark like a tunnel. Light at the far end illuminated a large rectangular box. Fear gripped me. I didn't want to go there. Mom nudged me forward, whispering, "It's okay Pat. You are going to meet all your Eastern aunts, uncles and cousins."

"But Mommy what's in that?" I whispered pointing toward the box.

"That's your Nana. She's asleep and on her way to heaven. It'll be okay. Just hold my hand."

Nana, my Dad's mother, had died. She lived in Brooklyn, New York. When Dad received the phone call notifying us of Nana's death, he insisted that Mom take Ellen, Maureen, and me to represent him at the funeral. Dad claimed that with the pear harvest upon us, he was too busy to go. I imagine Mom was excited at the prospect of seeing her dad, mom, and sister Charlotte again but was probably uncomfortable knowing she would have to make excuses to Dad's big family for his failure to honor his mother.

According to family lore, Dad was his mother's favorite of her 13 children. Nana often interceded between her son and her husband. Father and son had a rocky relationship as they worked together in their wholesale fruit business on the docks. I didn't remember Nana or my Grandfather, since we left New York when I was three. Our bookshelves and albums held pictures of Nana sitting under an umbrella with Ellen and Maureen at Coney Island Beach. I found only one or two rather formal pictures of my Grandfather tucked away in a family album.

Thirteen children and their families and friends made for a very large gathering at the viewing. My mother, sisters, and I stood silhouetted in the entrance. Folding chairs sat around the entire edge, filled with people of all ages whispering, "Look it's Em, Joe's wife and kids. All the way from Oregon."

Flying in a brand new United Airlines DC-6 four-propeller engine plane from Portland, Oregon to Washington, D.C. in 1948 was going to be exciting but first Dad had to deliver us to the airport, which was an adventure in itself due to recent flooding in the Portland area. Mom hurriedly packed and we were off on the three-hour rainy drive to the airport through the Columbia River Gorge. The narrow road, lined with masterfully worked stone guardrails, wound up and down the cliffs on the Oregon side of the Gorge. As we approached each of the seven tunnels along the way Dad tooted the car horn and we squealed with delight.

Around this time the Vanport flood had wiped out the transient wartime city of Vanport, Oregon, home to 40,000 people at its height. It was the aftermath of this flood that increased the drama of our trip from Hood River to the airport. Vanport's Post-war population was 18,500 people, 6,300 of whom were black. The city was located east of Portland. When Oregon was admitted to the United States in 1859, it was the only state whose constitution explicitly forbade black people from living, working or owning property within its borders. Until 1926, it was illegal for black people to even move into the state. Its lack of diversity was compounded by racial discord originating miles away and decades earlier: whites looking to escape the South after the end of the Civil War flocked to Oregon, which billed itself as a sort of pristine utopia, where land was plentiful and diversity was scarce. World War II changed all that. White males were drafted and mostly black men and women filled the gap, snapping up jobs that were previously not available to them. Completed in just 110 days, Vanport—comprising 10,414 apartments and homes—was mostly a slipshod combination of wooden blocks and fiberboard walls built to accommodate these new workers. Built on marshland between the Columbia Slough and the Columbia River, Vanport was physically segregated from Portland—and kept dry only by a system of dikes that held back the flow of the Columbia River.

Harsh winter storms left the mountain snow pack bloated, and warm May rains combined with the spring melt raised the level of the Columbia River to dangerous heights. By May 25, 1948, both the Columbia and Willamette Rivers reached 23 feet, eight feet above flood stage. Late afternoon on May 30, which happened to be Memorial Day that year, Vanport was inundated within 10 minutes. In less than a day, the nation's largest housing project—and Oregon's second largest city—was destroyed. The main Portland airport disappeared with the flood just days before our departure. When we arrived at the Portland airport, United Airlines rushed us and other passengers into a black limousine, dashed through flooded roads and fields, and shuttled us to the Troutdale airport 13 miles and 20 minutes away.

On our arrival, tall willowy airline stewardesses greeted us warmly, statuesque in their tailored, sea-green suits, perky caps and three-inch-high heels. I watched, transfixed as they balanced themselves during the bumpy flight. Air pockets were common, making the plane bounce dramatically, causing many passengers to make use of paper "barf" bags. Inflight meals, served on real china with heavy flatware and tiny little salt and peppershakers, tasted delicious if one's stomach settled enough to eat.

Mom impressed upon us the etiquette of dressing appropriately for transcontinental travel, regardless of how long the trip (ours was ten hours) or how uncomfortable the fashion. We girls wore matching green-checked suits made by Mom, white blouses with Peter Pan collars, white socks and patent leather Mary Jane shoes. Mom's ensemble included a very tight and restrictive girdle, nylons, heels, suit, hat and gloves. For years after, Mom reminisced about how she didn't get out of that girdle for two miserable days. Those rubbery restraints could put a stranglehold on a person.

We arrived at Arlington National Airport, outside Washington, D.C. in Northern Virginia, to spend a few days with my Dad's youngest sister, Aunt Dorothy, and her husband, Uncle Jonsie. Everyone at the Arlington house appeared somber and tearful, speaking softly. Nana had lived with them the last few years of her life. Eventually, we would all accompany Nana on the train to New York for her viewing, visitation, and funeral.

My first impressions of Uncle Jonsie have lasted a lifetime. He assumed the responsibility of keeping the kids entertained during the long hours of preparation and grieving. Always fascinated to learn what made people tick, he was interested at that time in hypnosis. I remember him sitting me in a big burgundy-colored wingback chair. He dimmed the lights and encouraged me to relax and keep my eyes on the gold watch he swung from a gold chain: back and forth, back and forth. He talked soothingly, melodiously. I don't remember anything else, but Uncle Jonsie gave me a healthy respect for hypnosis. In later years, as a young adult working in the Washington, D.C., area, I frequently used his skills to calm myself after a stressful day at the office.

On the day of the viewing and funeral, Mom urged me along the line of chairs filled with relatives and friends of the family. It seemed to take a very long time. I dreaded reaching the front of the room where Nana lay in that box, so I welcomed pauses as folks stopped us to ask, "How was your trip?" and "Where is Joe?" When they heard we had flown to the East Coast, everyone wanted to hear about flying.

Inevitably, we arrived at Nana's side. Mom held tight to my hand and whispered, "Pat, you stand on the kneeler while I kneel down, that way you can see Nana." I really didn't think I wanted to see Nana. "We'll say some prayers for her now."

Standing on my tippy-toes, my eyes barely reaching to peer over the edge of the coffin, I peeked in with dread, eyes squinting but expectant. There she lay in a black dress, illuminated by a halo of light, her hands peacefully folded on her stomach with a black rosary entwined in her fingers, a silver cross dangling. Flowers surrounded her casket, exuding a pungent, cloying smell.

So, this is what dead looks like. How will she get to heaven in that heavy box? I said a prayer that her guardian angel got her

26

there safely, and asked Jesus to take special care of Nana in heaven since Dad couldn't be there to help her on her way. I tugged a little on Mom's hand, wanting to leave.

We continued around the rest of the room, meeting everyone. Dad's brother Richard and his wife and daughter made a lasting impression on me. Uncle Richard fell somewhere in the middle of the thirteen Loschiavo children and, as we approached, Mom whispered, "Pat, Uncle Richard is a "deaf-mute."

"Mom, what's that mean?" I saw Uncle Richard and his wife make animated movements with their hands.

"It means they can't speak or hear so they use what they call sign language, spelling out words with their hands. Their daughter, Catherine, can hear and speak and she interprets what they want to say to us." Mom explained.

Uncle Richard appeared jolly and kind undeterred by his special challenges. He lifted me to his lap where I remember feeling safe and relaxed after the unnerving experience seeing my dead Nana. Uncle Richard taught me hand signs while Mom visited with his wife and daughter.

With the hard part behind us, we turned toward the Ridgewood area of Brooklyn to stay with Mom's parents in their row house. We had one month to explore the city and reconnect with relatives. Grandma and Grandpa Elser seemed as excited to see us as we were to see them. Last I saw Grandpa I was three and a half and didn't remember much but I found him wonderful and kind. I can still recall the lingering sweet smell of his pipe. He greeted me on our arrival with two things I had never seen before, both made by his own hand: my very own pair of stilts and a scooter equipped with a foot break. He made stilts for Ellen and Maureen too but I was the only one who got a scooter. Grandpa patiently helped us master skills for walking on stilts, interspersing lessons with trips to the corner store to buy penny candy and cream sodas. Sometimes Grandpa let me accompany him to the local pub on the opposite end of their block to kibitz with cronies.

Grandpa always expressed himself in a quiet soothing way that was very different from Dad's more insistent demand for respect.

Cars and trucks whizzed by Grandma and Grandpa's long and narrow row home, which rose three stories high. City living was exciting and very different from our western home. The kitchen and dining area sat belowground with an outside entrance. On that same underground level, Grandpa stored his workbench down a dark hallway, past a bathroom and small bedroom. There he crafted fine furniture. Wafts of his pipe smoke permeated everything, giving the home a cozy feel.

Up two steps, the back door led to their walled vegetable garden and the cages of Grandpa's pet homing pigeons. The second floor of their home included a separate street entrance. The living room faced the street and was equipped with a black-and-white TV, which we could watch as late as we managed to stay awake—a real novelty to the Higgins girls, since television had not arrived in the West. Next came a bedroom and then the formal dining room, with another bedroom all the way at the back of the house, overlooking the garden. Grandpa had converted the third floor into an apartment to rent for extra income.

The adventures we experienced during our month in the East left lasting memories. Aunt Charlotte, Mom's only sibling, was childless, and her nieces held a special place in her heart. One day, down the street from where she worked as an executive secretary in New York City, she treated us to lunch at the Horn and Hardart Automat on 42nd Street, a precursor to the fast food restaurants of today. The walls were filled with brightly lit, small glass doors, which were labeled with its contents. After Aunt Charlotte put coins in the slot by each door we selected, it magically opened, and out slid our sandwich and dessert.

That afternoon she bought tickets to a performance of the high-stepping Rockettes at New York City Music Hall. The music hall, the largest indoor theater in the world, also served as a movie theater and was huge. The stage held as many as fifty Rockettes in a straight line. Each dancer seemed identical to the next—in hairstyle, makeup, height and outfit. When they came on stage my heart raced as the fast-paced show unfolded without a single misstep. I was enthralled with the glitz, glamor, and beauty. Afterward, we three sisters gleefully lined up in the living room at Grandma and Grandpa's and worked to emulate the precision of those high-kicking, gorgeous women.

A Circle Line Boat tour around Manhattan Island afforded us views of many famous landmarks: the United Nations, Wall Street, and the Empire State Building, to name a few. We stopped at the Statue of Liberty, where we climbed all the way to the arm and crown on rather rickety steps. I remember losing my footing and sliding down several steps, terrified I would disappear into the depths before regaining a foothold.

As we walked into the sunshine from the dark interior of the statue, a television newscaster approached us. TV interviews were so rare in 1948 that he needed to explain the whole process before Mom allowed him to interview us for live TV. He thought we three girls were picturesque, dressed in matching checked suits, white socks, and paten leather shoes, with pigtails hanging down our backs. He seemed to think it newsworthy that we were in New York, all the way from the Wild West. During the interview we only said our names and ages, but Mom told more of our story. It aired that night on local news, and the Kellys, our next-door neighbors in Manhasset on Long Island before we moved to Oregon, saw the telecast and told us when Mom called them. It was truly thrilling!

Staying with Grandma Elser meant hugs that smothered me with love as she crushed me to her and gave me the safe feeling of being in a warm cocoon. I could do or say no wrong. Even at my tender age I recognized this cascade of tenderness from my grandparents as special and greedily soaked it up. I needed to tuck that cache of affection deep in my bones to offset painful things that happened at home.

For sightseeing outings, Grandma always packed a snack bag with yummy candies, cookies and nuts. One warm evening, a lady Grandma knew came knocking at the door bearing a long rectangular box. Grandma turned toward me and announced, "Pat, my friend has brought this special box for you." The box was almost as big as I. Carefully I knelt and placed it on the linoleum floor. Lifting the lid, I gasped.

"Oh, my! Grandma, it's a beautiful doll." I moved aside the white tissue and lifted her out of the box. She wore a navy blue dress, the collar trimmed with white lace, and a little white apron and blue bonnet to match. White socks and white rubber Mary Jane shoes adorned her feet. Porcelain skin shone in the fading light, and her huge blue eyes with long, blond eyelashes actually blinked. Grandma's friend worked in a doll factory and was able to get a special price. Grandma beamed with pleasure as I cuddled my new doll.

We ate several unique meals during our stay. Aunt Charlotte and her husband, Uncle Al, lived in an apartment in Jersey City so that Uncle Al could be close to his job as a firefighter. One evening, they invited us all for dinner. Aunt Charlotte was an accomplished cook, and Uncle Al was famous for his mashed potatoes. He claimed he used ice cream to make them delicious, smooth, and creamy, and I believed him long after I became a cook myself.

Another time at Grandma's, I watched in absolute horror as Mom ate a soft shell crab sandwich. She slapped an entire crab between two pieces of buttered bread and ate the legs, shell, and all, pronouncing it delicious...Yuk, I thought. Little did I know that, years later soft crabs in any form would become one of my favorite delicacies.

I was introduced to another lifetime food favorite on this trip: lobster, boiled to perfection, served with melted butter. Dad insisted that, while we were in New York, Mom contact the Catholic priests who married them. She did, and they treated us to a lobster dinner on the Jersey Shore. Seated at the long table, the waiter brought each of us a bib, even the priests, which I remember thinking was very funny. Steaming, huge orange

crustaceans were placed before us on platters. Fathers Harrigan
and McLaughlin patiently helped us crack and pick the succulent
meat from the shells to be dipped in the liquefied butter, then
devoured with relish. I quickly understood the need for the bibs:
lobster juice, lungs, and shells spurted everywhere. When we
finished, the waiter gave us each a warm, moistened terry-towel
with which to clean our butter-and-lobster slicked hands. This is a
savored memory.

This collection of summer experiences hangs in my
memory bank for more than sixty years. A first brush with death is
dramatic and memorable for anyone. But the uniqueness of our
whole trip East, without the worry of keeping Dad satisfied,
introduced me to a new, more carefree way of experiencing our
world. The juxtaposition of two men I met on this trip, Uncle
Jonsie and Grandpa, compared to my Dad, helped me subliminally
understand that men could be strong like Dad, but also
reassuring, complimentary and loving at the same time.

Faith and Fiction

I stood, hands together, fingers extended toward heaven. A pure, white Holy Communion dress tickled my boney knees. The white-net fingertip veil whispered at my elbows, and a gentle breeze fluttered in the cool spring air. Poised, breathless with excitement, we waited for the signal to walk down the center aisle of St. Mary's Roman Catholic Church on the Heights overlooking Hood River.

The small country church was filled to capacity with parents and siblings. The line moved forward, I in the middle, appropriate for the "H" in Higgins. We kept our eyes straight ahead or respectfully lowered, never daring to look side to side as we approached the altar to experience a momentous occasion in our Church life: the receipt of our first Holy Communion—-the body of Christ.

I was six years old, and this ceremony launched me on a circuitous path, pushing and pulling me along for the next 65 years as I struggled to find and keep my faith. In retrospect, many Church teachings revolved around what are called "sacred mysteries," accepted on faith. Being of a practical nature, I didn't spend a lot of time trying to solve these mysteries. Many of my thoughts, however, were spent agonizing on the "dos and don'ts" of sin and sex, as emphasized by the Church. These I did take seriously...too seriously.

Until modern times, most things were mortal sins: lying, cheating, gossiping, French kissing, eating meat on Fridays, skipping Sunday mass, not going to confession.

There were also venial sins equivalent to white lies, like keeping your fingers crossed when Mom asked if you snuck that candy bar from her stash. Mortal sins gave you a one-way ticket straight to hell: venial sins, a ticket to purgatory. In hell, you burned for eternity and had lots of company. In purgatory, you were between Heaven and Hell, waiting until you were purged of those not-so-bad sins and could then go on to Heaven. Those folks still living prayed for your soul to help speed you on your way. This method of praying often called for "indulgences," get-out-of-purgatory-free cards in the Catholic way of thinking. Indulgences forgive sins and are granted for specific good works and prayers. In retrospect it seems I spent an inordinate amount of time worrying about which kind of sin I might be committing. Guilt was a major player.

Dad, born Catholic, expected strict adherence to these rules from us, but applied a different standard for himself as evidenced during the ride home from Church as he criticized the priest's homily and anyone he didn't particularly like in the congregation. Poor Mrs. Zueba, for example.

"Now remember, when we leave church today, don't stop and chatter with Mrs. Zueba." Dad instructed. "That woman will talk your ear off and hold us up." I thought she was an attractive lady and friendly, but Dad didn't like her. I don't think he considered himself unchristian when he picked apart his fellow parishioners, nor did he consider the example he set for his children.

Mom, born Lutheran, converted to Catholicism to marry Dad; otherwise the thinking at the time was she would roast in Hell. She became devout, and both she and Dad gave many volunteer hours to the church. Dad sold the most tickets to the annual sausage dinner, which we all helped serve. He raised money for the new church and gave labor and materials toward its construction. Mom contributed to bake sales, rummage sales, and the women's sodality—a religious organization devoted to the Blessed Virgin Mary and good works. Mom also helped clean the church and taught Sunday school.

Absolutely nothing got in the way of 8 a.m. mass on Sunday mornings. Like the postal carriers, neither snow nor rain nor sleet forestalled this trip to church. Many times, in days before snow tires or studded tires, we pushed the car up icy hills, skidding down the other side. Roused from warm beds by 6 a.m.

Mom braided three heads of hair into pigtails and got herself ready.

"Pat, quit wiggling, you're only making it take longer," she often chided. "Your Dad's going to be laying on that horn any minute if we don't hurry." Mom sighed as I itched around on the bedroom vanity stool. I watched in the mahogany-framed beveled mirror as Mom tried to sort through my black tangles of thick hair. As she pulled, my eyes grew into huge, round blue orbs. I grabbed the sides of the stool and clamped my lips tight. I, the third and last head to braid beside her own, frequently brought Mom to wits end.

Dad sat in the car impatiently waiting with a slight smirk on his lips as Mom finished and approved each set of braids. We hustled out one by one. Dad honked the horn, as Mom was the last to join us. He seemed to take great pleasure in aggravating not only Mom but also the neighbors at that early hour.

Mom was dressed in a finely detailed navy blue suit she made from a Vogue designer pattern, and she accessorized with a white silk blouse, navy blue heels, hat, purse and white gloves. Mom was an accomplished seamstress with a real eye for style, and the clothes she made always brought compliments.

As she rushed down the sidewalk, Dad remarked on more than one occasion, "Look at that face on your mother. She's always making weird faces, and there's no pleasing her." He continued his obnoxious honking until Mom settled into the passenger seat. I could see her face written with frustration as she tamped down her anger. Years later she shared with me, "Pat, just remember that it's the little things that count. Your father gives me big and expensive gifts at Christmas and birthdays, but diamonds and Coach leather purses don't make up for those everyday digs and nasty comments. They speak the loudest and can be most hurtful."

Every Easter, we stopped at the local florist before Mass and Dad presented us with huge purple orchid corsages that drew lots of attention as we walked the church aisle to our pew near the front. The flowers were intended as a reward for fasting and sacrificing the forty days and forty nights of Lent preceding Easter. I usually gave up chocolate as a devotion and symbol of Christ's suffering. I always felt the gigantic purple flower perched on my small chest might swallow me whole before I could get home and eat the contents of my Easter basket. I saw the orchid as one of Dad's lavish gifts. It drew attention to him and his generosity as we paraded to our church pew, but it made me feel embarrassed and conspicuous. To this day I've never liked orchids.

Pecking Order

In 1949, the world felt quiet. Beyond the Higgins' orchard, far beyond any happenings I knew of at the time, President Truman raised the minimum wage to 75 cents an hour and America focused on getting back to work after the end of World War II. Television blared in many households, and the Columbia River Gorge and Hood River anxiously anticipated the TV's arrival. America watched and listened to baseball, the favorite pastime, with Joe DiMaggio becoming the first player to be paid $100,000 as he led the New York Yankees to win the World Series. In contrast to the upbeat outlook of the rest of the country, however, the Higgins' household smoldered that summer.

My place in the family pecking order afforded me preference as Dad's sidekick. Prior to first grade, Dad took me most places: riding in the truck and on the tractor, hanging on the fruit trailer piled with boxes, visiting fellow fruit growers, going on errands to town, or settling into his easy chair in the curve of his arm as he read *Jack and Jill* magazine to me. However, being the sidekick carried intrinsic burdens. The implicit requirement was to always do and be more in Dad's eyes. I ran like the Energizer bunny to please him, and it kept my stomach twisted. During our trip from New York to Oregon he started calling me "Butch" and the nickname stuck, however, I hoped he'd labeled me out of affection, rather than because he openly wished for a son.

Dad insisted we all wear braided pigtails. Every morning Mom patiently braided our hair along with her own. She wore her braids curled around her head like a crown, with a kind of fluffy puff of hair at her forehead. Our father proudly paraded us around the valley. Old photographs of us wearing matching outfits prove we were adorable.

Ellen entered high school at the end of that summer and Maureen followed the next year. They desperately wanted to get their pigtails cut into more fashionable, grownup bobs. Mom

36

readily agreed. She was six months pregnant and weary from dealing with braids every morning before school and church and the battles over weekly hair washing at the kitchen sink. Getting their braids cut at the
end of the current school year would give Ellen and Maureen all summer to work with new styles before school began in the fall.

Presented with this reasonable rationale, Dad refused. He loved his girls in braids. A change of this magnitude signaled they were growing into young women, a development Dad struggled to entertain. It heralded a decline to his iron-fisted control. Mom, who most often acquiesced to Dad's dictates, took her stand. She marched us off to Betty Bloom's beauty parlor around the corner in Odell, Ellen and Maureen to experience the thrill of this life-altering event and me to watch and learn.

In retaliation for the haircuts, my father began his "Campaign of Silence" against Mom that day, three long months of angry silence between our mother and father that did not end until the birth of Pete on August 30, 1949. The tension kept us strung tight, like fine wire on a violin. Mom valiantly continued running the household, cooking, cleaning, and caring for all. Still, the nerve-racking atmosphere persisted. When words needed to be exchanged, Mom and Dad employed one of us: "Butch, tell your mother that I want dinner on the table at 6:00 p.m.," or "Pat, tell your father that Mr. Morgan needs him to call about the tractor repair." They even erected a big blackboard on the wall in the kitchen to communicate unspoken words. Sprinkles of white chalk dust became a fixture in our lives, like fine sprits of acid slowly burning holes in the lining of our stomachs.

The siege blessedly ended when the last Higgins child was born. "It's a boy!" Dad shouted into the old, hand-cranked, party-line phone. The coming of the Christ-child could only have superseded Dad's jubilation at the arrival of Peter Charles Higgins, his long-awaited son. Peter's birth in the tiny Hood River Hospital completed my father's prescription for the Higgins family: three girls—Ellen 12, Maureen 10, the cherished son and me 7.

Dad's happiness and exuberance seemed strange. He behaved as though he alone had accomplished this miraculous feat. He smiled, laughed, and phoned everyone he knew to share news of Pete's birth. Blue, paper-ringed cigars were liberally distributed to Dad's male friends and neighbors. Our house had been shadowed and mute, drapes securely drawn against a possible intrusion for three months. This turn-about of open exhalation signaled a sea change. Pete's birth produced a forgiving euphoria in my father. Life in the Higgins household gained a semblance of calm. Enthralled with our little brother, the answer to our father's fervent prayers, we basked in a tentative peace.

Shortly after his birth, Pete developed a severe case of eczema over his entire body. Mom made splints out of tongue depressants and soft white flannel for Pete to wear on his tiny arms and to keep him from scratching himself bloody. For three years, Mom and Dad took turns walking the floor as Pete cried in their arms. Mom swore that Dad's "Campaign of Silence" during the end of her pregnancy caused Pete's affliction. Whatever the cause, a tense and weary atmosphere moved back in. The enduring effect that this period in our lives would have on me, and I am sure on my sisters, only unveiled itself as I progressed into my 30s and 40s. I forged an early commitment never to engage in silent treatments in any relationship, favoring open communication.

Eventually, it dawned on me that Dad read stories to Pete now and took him everywhere he went. I, after all, attended school. Pete was available. Strangely, I don't remember being consciously jealous. I liked taking care of Pete, and he *was* cute, unless things did not go his way. I can see him at about age three, dressed in his cowboy hat, spurs, chaps, and holster with two cap guns, riding his stick horse up and down our front sidewalk, shooting his gun into the air. "Wheehah" he'd shout as he galloped along. One time, the cap gun stopped sparking. Furious, Pete threw himself to the ground and banged his head repeatedly on the gray concrete sidewalk, wailing until he achieved the desired result—one of us picked him up, dusted him off, dried his tears, fixed the recalcitrant gun, and off he went until the next tragedy befell him.

As Pete grew older, we worked together in the orchard. He'd hang on my shoulder, peer up at me with his baby blues, and plead, "Butchie, I'm sooooo tired, please help me!" Nine times out of ten, I caved. The alternative was facing Dad's wrath because the young trees would remain choked with grass, brush strewn under the trees, or sprinklers unchanged to Dad's satisfaction.

During those years, I worked harder at everything I did in hopes of receiving acknowledgement, if not praise, from Dad. My days as sidekick had clearly ended. Whether at work in the orchard, at school, or at play, I failed to meet the standards Dad set. I often thought I had met the mark, like raising my math grade from a C to a B, only to be told, "Well, Butch, is that the best you can do?" This had me off and running again, trying to jump the new bar. For better or for worse, the pattern of always trying to do more in hopes of receiving acknowledgement or praise from Dad, was securely set and endured my whole life.

As the fifties roared on, I began a slow and steady battle to please Dad that could never be won. I am grateful now that neither Pete nor I carried much conscious awareness of the Higgins family dynamic at the time. Maureen and Ellen would soon move away, and years of travel and discovery lay ahead for me. I felt very inadequate in my new role—not quite a big sister, but certainly not the baby anymore. If I were going to be a sidekick to anyone, it would have to be to myself, and as things looked from that new vantage point, I sorely needed one.

Odell, Oregon

My memories of our early days in Odell are like conflicted weather patterns, stormy and scary one moment and a cerulean blue, filled with puffy, white clouds the next. Much like those skies, our family dynamic conveyed an aura of uncertainty. I found what solace I could among my playmates.

Morning chores included making my bed, scattering last night's garbage among the pear trees behind our house, gathering the paper trash, filling the burn-barrel, setting it on fire, and stirring to make sure it stayed lit. Then I escaped into a day filled with games and flights of fancy, a make-believe world and a blessing. Early on I became the organizer of our small group.

"Bye, Mom! I'm going to find Junie and play cowboy and Indians," I said one day.

"Okay. Have fun. Say 'hi' to Mrs. Fletcher for me," Mom said, then returned to cleaning up the breakfast dishes.

Junie Fletcher lived catty-corner to us off Davis Road. As I opened her front gate and started up the walk, I saw Mrs. Fletcher perched on her kitchen table. She was framed in a pool of sunlight pouring through the window. She tilted her face upward and supported herself with her arms, like she was on a sandy beach. She wore a colorful top with thin straps. I knocked on Junie's door.

"Hi Pat," greeted Junie, as she opened the front door wide.

"Junie, want to get some of the other kids and play cowboys and Indians?" I asked.

"Sure. Let me go tell Mom. Come on in," Junie said, as we skipped into the kitchen.

"Hi Mrs. Fletcher. Whatcha doing?" I asked, always inquisitive and chatty.

"Hi Pat," she drawled, "I'm sunbathin'. I do so miss maa Louisiana sun, you know." Mrs. Fletcher, Mercylin, was born and raised in Louisiana and met Bob Fletcher when he was stationed there during the war.

"Will you get tan through that window?" I giggled. She looked like a mermaid from the sea.

"I sure hope so. So what are you two up to today?" Her sweet, soft southern twang filled the kitchen.

"Junie and I want to round up some of the other kids for a game of cowboys and Indians. Then, can Junie come to my house for lunch so afterwards we can play dress-up?"

"Okay. Y'all have fun. Junie, you be home for dinnah." Post-World War II Odell, located in the center of the Hood River Valley, was a safe and secure place for us to roam free for the entire day. Odell High School, located across the street from our house, played a key role in our activities. We learned to roller skate on its wide, cement sidewalks, which were also suitable for rousing games of hopscotch and jacks. We often jumped rope, chanting at the top of our lungs, "Down in the meadow where the green grass grows." A grove of giant pine trees to the left of the school provided all the pine needles we needed to play "house." We'd sweep clean each room so the needles formed the walls of our make-believe kitchen, living room, bedroom and bath. When our "house" was built, we'd assign roles and act out imaginary families and stories.

I remember one particularly warm, sunny spring day before I started first grade, when I played tag with Billy Bob Rush on the green grass between the two high school buildings.

Somehow, I caught and wrestled five-year-old Billy Bob to the ground and kissed him soundly, to the delight and cheers of our high school audience. We presented quite a picture: me with black pigtails and a freckled face and Billy Bob, the cutest boy in the neighborhood, with luminous blue eyes and a shock of sandy hair. Years later, when I kissed a boy "for real," I still remembered that Billy Bob had been my first.

41

The high school grounds were also useful when big snows came and schools closed. The road crews piled all the snow in the high school parking lot. One year the snow piles peaked 10 and 12 feet. This signaled to all the kids in the neighborhood that the time for sledding, snow forts, tunnels, and a snowball fight was at hand. Days passed as we applied ourselves to these tasks, returning home each evening at dark: cold, wet, weary, and contented. Mom served up cups of hot chocolate and tasty meals. Surely, she hoped that peace would slide in along with us, like a runner to home plate, enveloping us as we ate dinner. I didn't have words for it at the time, but the insidious tension between Mom and Dad continued seeping into the fabric of our home. It silenced me. I knew I felt joyful and positive outside with my friends. Why couldn't that feeling follow me home?

In the summer time, we girls enjoyed the thrill of dressing up in Mom's beautiful gowns from her days dancing at New York City nightspots. The Stork Club, a New York City icon from 1929 to 1965, was where celebrities mixed. On our summer trip in 1948 to New York my Uncle Al had treated us to lunch at this luxurious watering hole. Now he was a top salesman for his company, entrusted with an unlimited expense account—a reality in those three-martini-lunch days. Even my young mind sensed the glitz and glamour of the stars that dined there that day. Seated on soft, cream-colored leather banquets, each female guest was gifted with a petite leather-wrapped lipstick and perfume embossed with the Stork Club emblem. Mine resides on my vanity to this day.

Mom stored her evening gowns in a trunk that lived in the attic of the little picker's shack near our house. Since I had been to New York and to those nightclubs, I set the scene. Junie and I dressed up for hours, swishing around the yard, wobbling in our too-big, too-high heels, pretending we, too, danced the night away or married the handsome prince. I imagine this activity gave my mother a few hours of peace, a valued tradeoff for allowing us freedom with her coveted treasures.

I still get a warm glow when I reflect on those hours. I picture myself in the silver lamé dress with a deep sapphire blue panel and train down the back—my personal favorite. Mom told me stories about the lovely sapphire and diamond bracelet that she wore with this dress, now kept securely in a safe deposit box at the Hood River bank. She shared how it made her feel special and beautiful. On banking days, when she had time, Mom took me into the vault and opened the safe deposit box. Digging through the stock certificates and important papers, she produced a long gray box. I stood on tiptoe and looked inside at the bracelet twinkling up at us, hinting at the glamour of days past. Sequestered in the tiny cubical, under a pool of light from the single bronze lamp, Mom looked wistful as she whispered stories to me in happy remembrance.

Around this time, a bout of the measles forced my sisters to accept my company. At that time, we slept in one big room. I don't recall who contracted the ugly spots first, but all three of us were kept isolated in the bedroom, darkened to protect our eyes, while the disease ran its ten-day course. The measles are a leveler. Each of us looked like a palate of red polka dots, trying not to scratch for fear of causing lifelong pockmark scars. Mom lovingly applied pink calamine lotion to soothe the itchiness, but it only did its job for a minute.

The most effective relief came when Mom entered our sick room to entertain us. She drew a towel over a lamp creating shadows and a halo of light. She then began to read "Little Women," and we escaped into an imaginary world of wonder. In the evening, Dad entertained us by making rabbit shadows and other figures scurry on the wall. Left to our own devices, we'd play jumping jacks, hopping from one bed to the other until we collapsed in gales of laughter. Pillow fights helped burn off our pent-up energy, and I reveled in the inclusion and the interlude of family harmony.

School Days

Elementary school began with Mrs. Scott teaching us to read *Run Spot Run*. We learned to count, do simple addition problems, and follow a daily routine. Mom volunteered as a lunchroom helper, and I liked seeing her there midway through the day. In third grade, Mrs. Curry became my teacher.

"Boys and girls, you're now in the third grade, and we're going to learn cursive writing. No more printing," Mrs. Kirby squawked from her perch in the front of the classroom. Her black, stringy, graying hair, pulled back into a bun at the base of her neck framed her wrinkled face. She looked like a great vulture. On the list of best-liked teachers in our small country school of six grades, Mrs. Kirby ranked last. She wielded a long wooden ruler and applied it liberally to anyone failing to follow her precise instructions. I sat in the middle row of wooden desks, three-quarters of the way back from the front of the room. Here, I thought, I could safely hide.

Mrs. Kirby screeched, "Take out your tablet of lined cursive paper and write your name on the top." She gave us a moment to complete the task. "Now we'll begin practicing the alphabet in cursive. Below your name I want you to copy the letters I have written on the board."

We did as instructed. I struggled to form the cursive letters and tensed as I discovered Mrs. Kirby towering over me. "Pat, what're you doing? Why's that pencil in your left hand?" she heatedly exclaimed. I perceived I must have been doing something wrong.

I mumbled, "I'm left-handed, Mrs. Kirby."

Up to that point in my short life, my left-handedness had never been an issue. Sometimes at the lunch table, if I sat next to a right-handed person and we bumped each other, we'd giggle, but no one had ever spoken like it was an affliction. Mom had

44

difficulty teaching me to tie my shoes because she was right-handed. We overcame that by getting Ellen, also left-handed, to teach me.

"Well, we'll just see about that," said Mrs. Kirby, pursing her skinny lips with determination.

I think I became her mission that year. She did not succeed in forcing me to write with my right hand. She did, however, make me stop writing with my arm and hand curved across the top of my paper to form my letters, as one often sees "lefties" do. Being singled out, ridiculed, and punished on a regular basis made its mark. I resisted the war on my left hand, only to endure the ruler as it left red welts across my knuckles. I vehemently thought, *I hate you Mrs. Kirby, I hate you, I hate you!* Tears welled, unbidden, granting her satisfaction.

By the time I reached high school, I forgave Mrs. Kirby's single-mindedness when I realized she did me a favor. Mrs. Kirby taught me how to adapt in a right-handed world and to write without smearing my words, especially when I wrote with a fountain or ballpoint pen. I also received less ridicule and teasing from fellow students than other "lefties" since I wrote in what was considered a "normal" way, just a different hand. Although I did not know it when I was suffering Mrs. Kirby's blows to my knuckles and ego, this ability to "fit in" would be of the utmost importance to me. Through junior high and high school, the need to conform rather than stand apart became a real tug-of-war for me.

As I approached junior high, a hushed curiosity about sex permeated my world. Tension remained at home, but now it also found its way into my small social circles and even the privacy of my own mind, as I often felt confused and conflicted by misinformation. Priests, nuns, and teachers perpetuated many legends in an effort to keep young adults on the straight path to a saintly life. For instance, girls were admonished when helping erase the black board: always clean from top to bottom, *never* from side-to-side. A side-to-side motion would "excite boys."

Another caution was not to wear shiny patent leather shoes, because the girls' panties would be reflected in the shoes and the boys would see. (My husband relates a time when he and his buddies peaked in on the girls at his Catholic grade school. An enthusiastic nun was teaching the girls to put their arms up, elbows out and pull back vigorously, chanting, "I must, I must, I must improve my bust. I better, I better, if I want to wear a sweater." The well-intentioned nun surely rationalized she was instructing this exercise in the name of good health. Or she may have thought her own figure inadequate as a young girl and didn't want her students to suffer the same—still, her efforts were a contradiction to the party line.) Sadly, I don't recall having the real facts of life explained to me. Consequently, any knowledge gleaned was by guess and by golly.

Even into my middle twenties, I lived in a cloud of fear, wondering what sex was all about, I was too intimidated and insecure to seek out the right answers, but based on the "facts" available, I understood that sex was *only* for making babies, but how that actually happened was still a mystery.

One night, I sat shaking and terrified on the edge of our bathroom tub. I discovered a dark stain in my panties. Certain I was dying, I called for Mom, who only said "Pat, don't worry about it. It's called a period. You're just growing up. Here, take this pad and wear it when you have your period every month. And don't forget to change it!" She quickly scuttled from the room, leaving me anxious as a mewling kitten. This was not the same mother who had patiently explained the rituals involved in applying makeup. I remember peppering her with questions about lipstick, mascara, eyelash curlers, and rouge, all apparently safe subjects.

What I didn't know at the time was that menstruation, a natural process, had to do with the unmentionable, sinful subject of sex. My sisters didn't know anymore than I, or else they were too self-conscious to explain it to me. I muddled through, believing all kinds of wild theories gleaned from snippets of

46

information from ill-informed friends: menstruation is a terminal disease; babies grow in their mother's stomachs (how they came out remained a mystery); sexual thoughts or urges are sinful, but I didn't know what constituted a sexual thought in the first place, let alone a sexual act.

Looking back I remember one day in junior high, we had an assembly. It might be fair to assume my enlightenment about sex began here, but that was not the case. "Sex Education" at my public school turned out to be like a scary fairy tale.

Girls sat in rows on tan, cold metal folding chairs, fidgeting in black and white saddle shoes, knee-high socks, pleated-plaid skirts, sweaters, and Peter-Pan blouses. Our principal, a scowling middle-aged woman, gathered us in the gym and proceeded to "enlighten" us on the dangers of sex.

"Girls, you must never sit on a boy's lap unless you've a book between you and the boy's lap," she said. I leaned over and looked down the row; relieved to see I was not the only girl embarrassed by this revelation. My friends squirmed, pink-faced, staring straight ahead.

"At school dances, you must keep a visible space between you and your partner...in other words, daylight!" I wanted to scream from embarrassment. Our principal continued: "You must be on your guard at all times because boys are only interested in one thing..." That "one thing" was never spelled out, but we knew it had to be bad.

In high school, a few of my friends became pregnant. My parents let us know this was the worst thing that could happen. It brought disgrace on a girl and her family. Even then, I still only had a glimmer of how pregnancy came about. Sinful thoughts about things like that meant a trip to the confessional at church, where I told the priest the sins I committed in thought and deed and requested absolution, promising never to do "it" again.

Junior high blazed on, and my emotions undulated like a seesaw. One minute I was up, the next, down. It was hard finding my place within the family and at school. I wanted to be included and yet, at times, wasn't ready for my siblings' more mature worlds. Ellen, Maureen, and Mom seemed obsessed with bras before I fully understood their purpose. A typical and frequent exchange with my sister Ellen, for example, went something like this:

"Ellen?" I would ask.

"Quit bugging me, Butch."

Annoyance radiated from behind her defensive shield, as I tried again to gain her attention. I finger-pinged the *Hood River News* that she had wrapped around her like a cocoon as she read. Ellen, the oldest, was **all** about Ellen. Little sisters were to be ignored as much as humanly possible.

"I just want to know if we're going to Kobergs Beach this afternoon," Kobergs was the place to go during the summer months. All the high school kids who weren't working other jobs met there to swim and water ski. The Columbia River water was so cold from ice and snow melt that our legs turned polka-dotted orange and blue.

"Maureen and I are going, but we don't want you tagging along," Ellen often said. She had recently gotten her license and was pretty puffed up by this new freedom. Sometimes Dad let Ellen drive us to the beach on the Columbia River, a mile east of Hood River, and I got to go along. Summer mornings were devoted to thinning pears or apples from 6 AM to noon, but afternoons gave me a free pass to hassle my sisters and with any luck, enjoy the beach.

Kobergs' had a glamorous history, was the place to be seen in the early part of the twentieth century. Young folks danced to live bands in a lovely stone pavilion, now in ruins, on the high cliffs overhanging the river. Kids braver than I dived off those cliffs into the cold, crystalline waters of the swift-flowing river that defined the borders of Oregon and Washington. Ellen and Maureen were among the diving divas. Until Ellen got her driver's license we were relegated to the public pool located in the Heights neighborhood of Hood River. Dad or Mom dropped us

48

off for swimming lessons in the morning and collected us an hour later. Mom returned us in the afternoon to the guarded pool to meet friends and swim with abandon. By the time Ellen passed her driving test, we were all excellent swimmers, and Ellen had taken a life-saving course. Her license allowed us to bypass the public swimming pool and eliminated Mom and Dad driving us to and fro. Those days at Kobergs when I was a pre-teen were mostly fun for me. Hanging out with my older sisters and their friends presented the opportunity to listen in on their world—much of which I didn't understand. I discovered that, if I questioned them about anything, the seemingly shocking realization that I was still there made them change the subject, leaving me in a state of confusion.

As the oldest child, Ellen experienced many negatives and positives in the Higgins household. Pictures abounded of a perfectly formed baby and toddler with huge green eyes and jet-black hair. Parents, grandparents, aunts, and uncles treasured her while we lived on Long Island in New York. A family legend from that time divulges a frightening drama that I think may have impacted her entire life.

One cold winter afternoon, Mom, Dad, and little Ellen traveled across New York's Triborough Bridge in their relatively new car. It was the winter of 1939. Dad sat alone in the front seat, driving. Safety locks, seat belts, and car seats were but inventions of a distant future. Ellen, an inquisitive two-year-old just beginning to explore her world, sat in the back seat along with newborn Maureen, whom Mom cuddled in her arms. Mom's attention remained riveted on her blond, curly-headed addition to the family. I see in my mind's eye Ellen fidgeting, jealous of the attention showered on Maureen. Slyly, she fiddled with the car door handle. A gust of winter air rushed in. Mom screamed, "Joe! Stop the Car! Ellen's fallen out!"

"What? Christ! Oh my God, she's going to be killed!" he yelled, jammed on the brakes and leaped out into oncoming traffic. He frantically waved his arms for cars to stop and ran to

Ellen. He scooped her up as a produce truck bore down on them, screeching to a halt with only feet to spare. Dad carefully turned Ellen over and her bloody face made his heart stop. The Triborough Bridge's steel surface grids were imprinted on her delicate skin and had cut her face as she fell head first from the moving car. "Em, we've got to get her to a doctor." he bellowed. The ride to the hospital was wrought with tension, as they fretted over the seriousness of Ellen's injuries.

The doctor pronounced that Ellen's winter snowsuit had saved her from serious injury. It provided a cushion and allowed her to bounce when she fell to the bridge from the car. To this day, Ellen carries a small black mark high on her cheek. The family revisits this incident whenever Ellen's behavior is in question and we are trying to figure out why she does what she does.

For instance, I still wonder about a mind-boggling incident the year I was a new sophomore in high school and Ellen attended Marylhurst College on the outskirts of Portland. Dad and Mom took all of us to Long Beach on the Washington coast for a weekend of clam digging. The siblings enjoyed these outings even though it meant Dad woke us at the beginning of every low tide, usually at 3 or 4 am. It was pitch black on a fog-damp morning—the best time to get to the beach and catch our limit. We competed, trying to be the first to get our daily 24 razorback-clams. The clams were slippery buggers and strong, fast diggers. Carrying clam shovels and buckets, we stomped the sand with bare feet, watching to see if any of our stomps produced air holes which indicated there was a clam beneath. Quickly, we shoveled two or three scoops of sand, dropped to our knees, and started dog-digging frantically with our hands until we fingered the sharp shell of the tunneling clam. Getting a secure hold on a clam while it suctioned in the opposite direction took persistence, but little skill. Friendly camaraderie among the six of us prevailed as we focused on a common goal. Dad encouraged us "Dig Butch, Dig...That's a nice one, Ellen," positive comments rarely heard at home.

On the second day of our trip, Ellen's college friend Shannon visited from her home in nearby Olympia, Washington. Shannon's dad was a successful doctor, which absolutely impressed Dad. Shannon planned on attending the University of Vienna, Austria, during the second semester of her junior year and wanted Ellen to go with her. I remember Shannon as a beautiful brunette with expressive brown eyes. She dazzled Dad, and he agreed to let Ellen accompany her to Europe the following year. Ellen, already bored with clamming, hatched a plan to go back to Olympia with Shannon. Their plan included taking me along since my age of sixteen fell right between Shannon's younger brother and sister. I could hardly believe my good luck. Ellen actually wanted me along. In reality, I'm sure Ellen knew her chances of selling her scheme to our parents improved if she included me in the deal. We planned to take the bus back to Hood River from Olympia.

Shannon's mom welcomed us warmly into her grand home. At dinner the room filled with raucous laughter, political debate, and a clear signal that the rules were loose and liberal. James, the only son and older than I, had a driver's license. He appointed himself my personal tour guide of the Olympia hotspots. *Wow!* I thought *a real date, with a doctor's son who actually seems interested in me. Ellen must not think I'm such a tag along kid after all. Gosh, I hope I don't do anything dumb.*

James drove us around in his pickup truck for an hour, pointing out the brightly illuminated capital building and other sights to me. Songs of the day wafted from the radio like "Love Letters in the Sand," "Little Darlin'," and "Young Love." We made small talk, but I was nervous and had trouble focusing. Finally, James parked beside an abandoned warehouse, and he came on really strong. Sliding me over next to him, his arm slipped around my waist, and he nuzzled my neck. His lips creeped progressively toward mine. My thoughts screamed, *Oh, my God! This is way too fast, what is he doing? We hardly know one another... I think I am in way over my head.*

"James, James, stop … please, wait a minute." I gasped sliding my arms between us, trying to create space.

"What's a matter? You're not going to get all cold and frosty on me, are you?" he said, with a tinge of annoyance. "You're a grownup girl, right?"

"I think we should go back … to your house, please." Little did I know what waited? I was to sleep with Meredith, James' younger sister, in her double bed. That much seemed fine. But James and Meredith had concocted an insidious plan at my expense. Meredith and I talked and giggled, exchanging confidences. I drifted into sleepy dreams and then sensed a presence, a pressure actually, curving into my back, stroking. In alarm, I bolted up and turned to find James where Meredith had been.

"What're you doing? In my bed!" I felt frightened of this obviously experienced male with one thing on his mind. I wouldn't need to ask my older sisters about that "one thing" any more. I didn't understand the technicalities, but I felt the reality of it right next to me in bed and wanted nothing to do with it. I also felt hurt and betrayed by James and his sister, unsure what to do or how to get James out of the room.

Somehow, I did get him to leave, and the first thing next morning I ran to Ellen, explaining what happened. She saw how shaken I was, as I pleaded with her to take me home.

"Why? Why do we have to leave and go home? He didn't hurt you, did he?" Ellen said trying to calm me down.

"Well, no, he didn't. But both of them were so sneaky about it. I don't feel safe staying here another two nights having to fight James off. I thought you'd understand." I felt aghast that she could be so obtuse. Where was her sense of loyalty? Even if I was annoying, surely her loyalty remained with family.

"Pat, Shannon and I had a lot of fun last night with her friends, and we've plans to meet them again tonight. Can't you just hang in there till we're supposed to go home Sunday?"

"Ellen, that's two days away! No, I can't. You put me on the bus, and you can stay if that's what you want, but I can't stay in this house" I paced the room in obvious distress. I stood my ground, and we boarded the bus for home two days early. Ellen was furious.

I chalked up moments of disconnect like this as yet another result of the "Triborough Bridge bump-on-the-head incident," in fairness to Ellen, we mimic our elder's behaviors. I know I copied Dad's biting sarcastic humor, which was always hurtful to the recipient. Ellen, as the first child, was surely more impacted by Dad's moods and negativity. Her behavior may have been her defensive shield against what she witnessed.

Although sisters, we each interacted with Dad differently. Ellen could charm Dad, while Maureen knew best how to circumvent his watchful eye. Family called her. "Reen", or "Reenie," and her legion of friends called her "Mo." She was smart and gutsy, and her circumvention of house rules involved a sleight of hand. Well into my thirties, I remember being amazed when Reen finally confided how she got around Dad's hard-and-fast rule of "be home at midnight."

"So Butch, what I'd do was get my date to stop his car at the end of the sidewalk before curfew with headlights off. I'd hop out and run on the grass up to the front porch so I wouldn't make noise."

"Weren't you scared," I asked.

"You bet I was, my nerves were jangled and I quivered with fear of being caught."

"What did you do then?"

"I twisted the porch light bulb off and then dashed back to my date's car. I don't think Dad ever figured it out."

"Reen, that was really a fearless thing to do, I know I'd never have had the nerve to pull it off. But you know, I think Dad might have guessed what you were up to but chose to amuse himself by watching your deception."

When Dad laid down a decree, Reen's acquiescence just *seemed* to Dad (and the rest of us) that she would obey his edict without question. On the other hand, unlike either of my sisters, I preferred letting Dad know where I stood and why. This approach, however, caused me a great deal of angst, much to Dad's enjoyment.

For years, I felt alone in the Higgins household. Only as I became a young adult and moved away did I begin to understand. The web of ridicule and anxiety had trapped each of us in different ways. We all bore scars.

I always thought Maureen and Ellen enjoyed a close relationship. Growing up, they slept in the same room, shared the same friends, and participated in the same sports: skiing, swimming, and tennis. They even exchanged clothes and jobs around the house and orchard. When I mentioned my impression to Maureen years later, I learned differently. "No," she said. "We were close in age and only a year apart in school. That's why we ran with the same crowd. But we never shared confidences, and I never felt we were particularly close." In spite of that, Maureen is the glue that has held our family together over the years, striving to keep connections amongst siblings.

When it came to his son, Dad was an especially stern taskmaster. "Pete, what's the matter with you? You've been sitting at this desk for two hours and accomplished nothing. Are you dumb or just lazy?" he'd ask. Dad grew continually frustrated by Pete's seeming inability to efficiently tackle homework. He exploded, spewing hurtful and demeaning comments at his longed-for son, who failed to meet his expectations. Besides mental abuse, I stood witness to whippings that resulted in welts wherever the black five-tailed strap connected. I remember shouting at Dad to stop, trying to protect my brother. I don't think I succeeded. These torturous scenes never produced Dad's desired results. They did succeed in driving Pete farther away however, and to this day I wonder how he would tell the story of being the chosen one.

Mom remained in a constant state of agitation, always the go-between, mitigating abusive episodes. In the aftermath, she tried comforting Pete and, in the process, denigrated Dad. Both she and Pete saw themselves as victims with few options. Our home trembled with tension, and I cannot remember Pete as happy, only troubled. Dad loved sports, and Pete played everything, excelling in track. Mom never missed a sporting event. But I don't think Dad ever went to see his son compete, probably fearing disappointment.

One night I lay on my bed curled around my pillow as I listened hard to the angry voices on the other side of the wall. Mom and Dad had been fighting a lot lately, but it seemed to get worse after Maureen left for her first year of college. It was 1956, and I entered Wy'East High School as a freshman. Before Maureen's departure I shared a room with my brother Pete. Now I enjoyed my own room right off the kitchen. That night, hearing the ugly, spiteful words of my parents, I questioned the advantage. Eventually, it quieted. Dad always went to bed no later than nine, so I was pretty sure that's what had ended their fight.

I heard a tap on my door, and Mom entered, silhouetted in the soft lamplight.

"Pat, I've got to talk to you." Mom said softly. I held my breath, afraid of what was coming. "You know Dad and I aren't getting along?" She waited for my nod. It was all I could offer. My voice had taken fearful flight. My heart beat so hard I thought it would jump out of my chest. "I'm going to leave your father..."

"Oh" I squeaked.

"I'm not sure when," she continued, "but I'm leaving and felt you should know. You're going to have to choose whether you stay here with Dad or come with me."

Tears streaked down my cheeks. "Oh, Mom, no."

"You don't need to decide tonight. I'll let you know when you do." She said, and tears welled in her blue eyes as she kissed me on the forehead and slipped out.

Devastated, I sobbed into my pillow, rifling my frightened mind for whom to choose. I knew I wanted to be with Mom but if her leaving meant moving, changing schools, finding new friends—oh it was a terrifying prospect. Finally, sleep granted me release. I never had to make that choice but the anticipation caused me hours of anguish.

During my high school years, Pete grew old enough to work with me in the orchard. The outdoors still offered me a sense of freedom, but as I matured, I noticed this feeling was transient. As I worked, hoeing weeds away from young pear trees, I imagined a happy home, brimming with warmth and laughter, just like in the pine-needle homes my friends and I built during primary school recess. While I liked having someone with whom to talk and share the work, I felt conflicted about Pete's presence. He had little staying power and seemed to frequently find a way to off-load his share of the work. We carried on. Pete learned the art of manipulation often laced with sarcasm, just like Dad. I continued developing a driving work ethic in search of praise that never came.

Freshman Shadows

Ill-prepared to leave the relative security of small-town Odell for my destination 1,500 miles east in Denver, Colorado, made me anxious. In the fall of 1960, I was to begin attending a Catholic women's college run by Lorentine nuns. The scariness of leaving home lessened somewhat when I received a letter from my "big sister." The college, Loretto Heights, assigned an upperclassman to guide and orient each incoming freshman. Sue, also an Oregonian, became my beacon in the new, almost grownup world. Through an exchange of letters, Sue kindly answered my questions and assured me that she'd help me navigate the uncertain waters of being so far from home in a big new city and school.

In an effort to ready myself for this upcoming adventure, I accepted a new challenge in sophistication. As a thin wisp of smoke floated toward my open bedroom window, I pursed my lips, wrinkled my brow, and shivered, concentrating to suppress a cough as I tentatively sucked on the filter of my Salem Menthol cigarette. The tip provided the only illumination on this cold and snowy night in 1960. I hoped my room at the opposite end of the house from my parents would allow me the needed privacy to accomplish my goal of learning to smoke. I needed to perfect this ability without tearing up or coughing uncontrollably. It was unthinkable that I might begin my freshman year without these accomplishments.

My parents and their friends smoked for as long as I could remember. Everybody in the movies, television, offices, restaurants, doctors' offices, and hospitals smoked. If you didn't smoke, you were definitely not "with it." Sophisticated women blew gentle streams of smoke into the faces of men whom they found attractive. Handsome men smoked heavy-duty brands like Camels or Marlboros and they carried lighters like six-shooters to whip out and light a lady's waiting cigarette as subtle invitation in social settings. If a man wasn't the rugged athletic or outdoors type, a pipe was a more distinguished choice. My Dad often smoked a pipe, and I can still smell that warm, rich scent that surrounded him and made him seem less austere.

For weeks, as soon as Mom and Dad went to bed, I unearthed the pack of cigarettes hidden at the back of my desk, doused the lights, and quietly opened the window. The air was frigid, but I was in training. Taking a deep breath, I put the filtered end of the menthol Salem between my lips, struck a match, and dragged. Fits of coughing ensued as I fanned the smoke to keep it going out the east window. I smothered my face in my pillow to suppress the racking coughs. As they subsided, I listened intently, holding my cigarette out the window; my heart beat like a snare drum until I assured myself that the house remained quiet and Mom and Dad still slept, unaware of my subterfuge. I rebelled against the rule that I was not to smoke. Both my older sisters smoked, and I was going to college in the fall. I was willing to take my chances.

Each evening it was the same. With time the coughing and tears subsided, and I could inhale and even let the smoke curl out through my nostrils. Soon I perfected the smoke ring, and I knew I was ready to begin my college career.

By the time I graduated college in 1964, I was smoking a pack a day and had blown smoke into countless handsome faces. Within five years, the Public Health Cigarette Smoking Act passed Congress. It imposed a ban on cigarette advertising on television and radio and required the Surgeon General produce an annual report on the latest scientific findings on the health effects of smoking. I remember watching the Surgeon General on TV warning the American public of how bad smoking was for one's health. Nancy, my roommate and I decided to quit cold turkey.

By this time, I was smoking a pack and a half a day. Quitting without prep or preamble proved to be a daunting challenge. During the initial stages of withdrawal Nancy and I were short-tempered and bitchy for more than a month. We quibbled over silly things. One incident that stuck in my mind occurred over making salad. Nancy was pretty much the boss. She owned the house and set the rules and my designated job that evening was to clean the romaine lettuce, dry it and get it into the salad bowl. I accomplished the first two steps successfully and was starting on the third as a very agitated Nancy appeared by my side.

"What're you doing to that romaine?"

"I'm cutting it up for the salad. What's the matter, Nancy?"

"You should never cut lettuce. Cutting it bruises the leaves," she shrilled.

"So, you want me to do what?" I could feel my blood pressure amp up a few notches and my face reddened with puzzling embarrassment. I had been cutting romaine for salads since I was a wee one, and my mom found it perfectly acceptable.

"I want you to tear the leaves into bite size pieces. Everyone knows you should tear the leaves, not cut them." Mortified, I did as instructed and chalked the intensity of this exchange to nicotine withdrawal.

For the most part, Nancy and I kept each other moving toward our goal with positive reinforcement, but that first month was a struggle. It was liberating to make it through another day without lighting up. Nancy and I succeeded while gaining ten pounds due to renewed appetites. Food tasted so good, and I don't think I ever shed those pounds. Besides the pounds, I also grew in self-determination and fortitude. I no longer needed to immediately light up with my first cup of morning coffee, in social situations, or with a cocktail. I faced the monster and conquered the addiction only to unveil another unattractive trait— intolerance. Now I could not stand the smell of nicotine, cigarette smoke, or dirty ashtrays. I clearly saw smoking as a destructive and filthy habit and felt embarrassed to have been held in its grip.

With smoking tucked in my bag of tricks I was ready for Mom to take me to college. In late August of 1960, Mom and I drove up the circular road to the Loretto Heights admissions office, indeed located on the "heights." The campus's majestic buildings, constructed of red rock, looked out over the city of Denver to the east and framed the Colorado Rockies to the west, a breathtaking panorama engendering confidence and trust. The Lorentine nuns seemed gregarious, welcoming, and down to earth. Sue, my assigned college big sister, greeted us with a tour of campus, pointing out the student union and cafeteria, the chapel, and my dorm—things a freshman needed to know. She managed, at the same time, to reassure my mother that I was in good hands.

Those first weeks and months of college life proved exhilarating and confounding. I fell in with a great group of freshman girls in my dorm. We enjoyed newfound independence, exploring college activities like dances with our "brother" school, Regis College for men, just a few blocks away. Ranked high on our list of preferences were: drinking Coors light beer (referred to as three-point-two beer and legal in Colorado for eighteen-year-olds), learning the Twist (a new dance craze), and dating men.

School rules strictly dictated our comings and goings. Dates could meet us in our dorm lobby but not go anywhere else in the building. Dating curfews and decorum dictated how a "Heights" lady conducted herself. She best remember that she, as a good Catholic woman, always represented the school, which Denver society held in high esteem. Translation: Denver society contributed lots of money to Loretta Heights.

The dating scene was fun. Although not as naïve as when I had listened to my mom and sisters talk about bras, I was still clueless and nervous about how far I could go with a boy. Up to that point dodging advances and saying "no" to a too-eager boy had worked for me. Dances at the Air Force Academy located just sixty miles south of Denver were especially exciting. Our cadet dates and we Lorentines were transported to and from the Academy by a special Air Force bus. Those cadets, so handsome in their blue dress uniforms, really turned a girl's head.

Sue gave me her undivided attention, almost to the exclusion of her own friends. One fall evening I found her waiting for me outside my dorm room as I returned from a date. As I approached, Sue straightened from her slouch against the wall and peppered me with questions about what happened. I sensed something off-kilter and felt my stomach clench with nervous anticipation.

"So, Pat, how was it?" she asked.

"It was a lot of fun, Sue. We went dancing at that three-point-two bar down South Federal Boulevard," I said.

"You look flushed. Did he kiss you?" Sue appeared unnaturally curious, even for a big sister, standing close in my space, a restraining hand on my forearm.

A knot tightened in my stomach, "Well ...yes ..."

"Did you like it?" she probed, her eyes boring into me.

Looking down, embarrassed now, I tried to edge away, "Yeah, I did." I knew the conversation wouldn't end unless I made some excuse, "I have to pee. Night." And I skittered down the hall.

I trusted Sue, so although I found her interrogations puzzling, I put it out of my mind. Perhaps she was just being overprotective.

At some point, Sue encouraged me to go on a school-sponsored weekend ski trip to Aspen. Skiing the high peaks of the Rockies in Colorado was magically addictive, plus we received college credit to participate in the ski program. This trip presented an opportunity not to be missed.

Unfortunately, I don't remember the skiing. Sue arranged for us to room together, an experience that ravaged my naiveté. I realized I was in way over my head. My experiences were limited to passionate kisses and some light touching like in that Olympia pickup truck. Any hand that threatened to cup or caress my tiny breast was instantly stopped—discovery of my padded bra was too mortifying. Now, in that dark lodge room, Sue professed her love for me and insisted I trust her to satisfy me sexually, better than any man. Not only was I ill equipped to deal with what I perceived as a threat, I didn't even know what sexual satisfaction meant for me. Did women do that with one another? Sue began to kiss and caress me. I was ridged, stiff, and scared.

The weekend could not end quickly enough for me. Sue did not want to join the rest of those on the trip, and I felt caught. I knew intrinsically that her advances were not right, but I struggled to know what to do. Sue was my Big Sister, after all. She said going with girls was all right—but not to talk to anyone about it. It did not feel right. It felt wrong. I was confused, embarrassed, and deeply ashamed of my acquiescence. Sue shadowed my every move. She questioned everything I did and felt. I dared not talk to my parents. Surely, they had never run into anything like this. Nor could I talk to my friends, or anyone I knew. I felt very scared and alone. Then, I realized: go to confession … talk to the priest …

I knew the sacrament of Penance allowed me to talk to God through the priest. He would listen to my sins, and if I sounded sincerely sorry, on behalf of God, the priest would forgive and absolve me. This was the Church's ritualistic way of pardoning mortal sins and returning the penitent, me, to a state of grace. I had been taught that if I followed the formula, I would escape the fires of Hell. First, I examined my conscience. This frightened me even more, because somehow, I felt complicit. Maybe from the way I looked or acted, Sue thought I wanted her attentions. I proceeded to the second step, walking into that dark, narrow box called the confessional, and told the priest.

My sweaty hands tented in prayer as I knelt in the confessional, expecting the priest to open the small-screened window. The dank smell of previous sinners pressed in against me as I waited in that upright coffin. My fear escalated with each passing second. I trembled, trying to build my confidence.

The slide covering the window quietly swished open. Voice quivering, I made the sign of the cross and began.

"Bless me Father for I have sinned. My last confession was six weeks ago." As I unburdened myself, I sensed the priest behind the screen where he sat stoically, hearing my concluding prayer. "I'm sorry for these and all my sins."

I expected a shocked reprimand followed by some sympathetic counsel. What I received in his modulated but firm voice was his blessing and admonition to "go and sin no more." Then he raised his hand, made the sign of the cross, and gave me an easily accomplished penance: "For your penance say five Hail Marys and three Our Fathers." He briskly shut the confessional window.

In retrospect, I think I was too intimidated by this authority figure to ask for more. He was faceless behind that screen. Perhaps given my fumbling way, he did not grasp my need for counseling and maybe punishment. Was this behavior to which I just confessed such a common occurrence in a women's college that it was treated as a trivial matter?

Sue and I made it through the rest of that Aspen skiing weekend but not without awkwardness. I avoided her the remainder of the school year. I felt beset with doubts—had I abandoned a friend? Sue presented me with dilemmas much larger than those I had ever found in the orchard. Disillusioned by my own church, I floundered until gaining the grit and maturity to deal with Sue on my own. What she offered was not in my best interests and wrong for me. It took many more years before I understood that I was not to blame, that her actions were demanding and controlling. Only through the counseling of a good psychologist when I was in my fifties, did I manage to look at this deeply hidden guilt.

I had tamped the fear and misgiving about my own sexuality far down in my subconscious. Mining those depths proved painfully hard work. However, the clarity and peace it brought me was like a lily opening to the morning sun. Regardless of sexual orientation, actions such as I'd experienced with Sue are unconscionable by the very fact that they are unwanted and predatory.

The Twist and Truth

Penny, my college sophomore roommate, was a life force in her own right. She tackled everything with gusto mixed with a little piss and vinegar. Penny was a petite, striking blue-eyed blond—until the day she decided to become a blue-eyed brunette like me because she thought we'd have more fun. It was hard for me to imagine having more fun or being better pals. Penny sang like a bird, and I loved to hear her belt out a song. I couldn't carry a tune if my life depended on it. In fact, at home I was laughingly sent out to the orchard if I attempted to sing along to tunes on the radio. Penny was sought after to perform in all of Loretto Heights' musical and choral productions that year. We supported each other in our respective studies, although Penny was the brighter student, quick to grasp the nature of a problem.

January semester exams were behind us. The Institute of European Studies (IES) accepted me to attend my junior year at the University of Vienna, Austria. Penny shared that she wouldn't be returning to The Heights next year either.

"What're you going to do, Penny? I asked.

"I know you're going to find this hard to believe, but I'm entering the convent," Penny said with a deadly serious expression.

"You can't be serious," I protested.

"I'm very serious. I've been thinking and praying about this for quite a while, and I've talked with Sister Jean D'arc about it. She thinks I've a calling. I feel in my heart it's what I need to do."

"You could've fooled me! All those stories you told me about Christmas vacation in Sandusky, Ohio. My gosh, Penny, you turned the place on its ear—dating, drinking, dancing, and making out with anything in pants," I laughed. Penny giggled too, remembering. "Are you sure about this?"

"I really am," she said. "I'll go into the Lorentine's novitiate in St. Louis in June for my training. But I think you should come home with me over the Easter break. I've told all the guys back home about you, and it'll be sort of a last fling before I enter. What'd you say?"

"I say let's do it!" We immediately began to make our travel plans for Easter break.

Spring warmed Penny's hometown of Sandusky and we enjoyed ten, fun-filled days and nights. We danced the newest dance craze, The Twist, performed by swiveling our hips. It became popular after Chubby Checker danced the Twist while singing the song of the same name on the *Dick Clark Show* in August of 1960. I couldn't carry a tune, but I had rhythm and loved to dance. Every night we danced, almost till we dropped. On our last evening in Sandusky, I managed to twist my tired knee right out of its socket. The alcohol level in my system helped to deaden the pain, but by morning my knee was swollen like a football and blazed with pain. The 22-hour drive back to Denver has been blocked from memory. Once in the college infirmary, I started a costly therapy and pain-killer regimen, much to Dad's chagrin.

As soon as I returned home for summer break Dad wanted an explanation of exactly how I'd hurt my knee. When I told him he said, "Didn't you twist it getting out of the back seat of the car?"

"No, I just told you I twisted it out of its socket on the dance floor."

"Butch, tomorrow we're going to see our insurance agent, and I want him to hear that you did this while getting out of the car."

Bewildered, I said, "Dad, that's not the truth. I can't tell him that. Why would I?"

"I'll do the talking," he said gruffly. "I want the insurance to pick up the tab for your medical bills, so it had to happen while you were getting out of the car."

The next day, we drove to the insurance agent's office in silence. While Dad talked, I watched the kind agent as he listened respectfully to my father's claims.

"I'm so sorry you had this mishap, Pat. I hope your knee has healed, and it's getting back to normal?" He asked.

Eyes downcast, face red with shame, I mumbled, "Yes sir." I willed him to understand the truth. I thought he might, as I chanced a glance into his knowing eyes.

"Your Dad's been a good and loyal customer, Pat. I'm going to give him some claim forms to take home and fill out. Once complete, just mail them back in, and we'll take care of your claim."

At home, Dad sat me down at the old Royal typewriter and directed me to complete the forms. Stubbornly, I made him dictate the answers, as I pondered this deceit and the lesson learned.

Travel Is Broadening

Salty air teased my nose as students waited anxiously at the ocean liner's rail for the loud blast. We were underway! Aunt Charlotte and Uncle Al looked like miniature dolls as they waved from the New York City pier below. I waved in return, shouting, "Goodbye, thank you for a wonderful send-off!" The farewell had included a week in New York City. As a college student entering my junior year, I felt like a fledgling bird ready to take wing, all thanks to my childless Aunt and Uncle who doted on me. That week, they squired me about to famous nightclubs like the Stork Club and the Copacabana, Broadway plays and fine dining. I experienced the charged aura of the most famous city in the world. Skyscrapers stood so tall and majestic they hid the sun. Everywhere, people rushing. Horns blaring. Breaks screeching. Chatter, chatter, chatter. And an excess of conflicting smells wafted over me: delicious sweetness from a bakery, the caustic sour of the subway, salt of sweaty bodies on an August afternoon. A crush of thousands of people moving with great purpose to some destination only known to them. All this, just prior to sailing to Europe in 1962 on the Statendam for my junior year abroad.

Waving at the ship's rail, I sent a silent prayer heavenward. I had made it this far—a real struggle. While pushing away from the dock, memories pulled me back in time. In the Higgins household, "going to college" carried indisputable clout. An alternative was never offered or discussed. My responsibility to achieve decent grades in high school came first and foremost so that this dream would be realized. I got better than passing grades, not really knowing how to study effectively. Starting college, I felt totally at sea, the academics above my head. That first year, I ended up on probation.

As sophomore year began, my objective became to study abroad with IES. That accomplishment was entirely in my hands. I needed to take my average from a D to a B by the end of the first semester—a tall order. Something in me told me I could attain it; after all, the brass ring promised a year in Europe!

After every class I returned to my dorm room and transcribed notes on my trusty Royal manual typewriter. During exam week, I sequestered myself in our dorm broom closet. Surrounded by dust and wet mops, buckets and brooms, I single-mindedly focused on preparation for the next exam. In that tiny closet, I could see myself standing on the deck of an ocean liner, tasting the briny air, as sturdy tugboats nudged our ship to sea. I formed this picture and desire from the exciting stories my sisters told when they returned from studying in Europe. I was determined to do the same. And here I was on the deck of this beautiful ship, heading out of New York Harbor to sea and a grand adventure.

We were all dressed in suits, which was customary in the 1960s. I wore a chic gray pinstripe that Mom had altered to fit me perfectly. She also insisted on giving me my first-ever perm and as the salty sea air enveloped us my hair became an unruly frizz.

Our group of 100 college sophomores and juniors destined for the University of Vienna, Austria, stood aboard the Statendam as it prepared for its journey across the Atlantic to Southampton, England. Collectively, we bid farewell to friends and relatives, to our country, to the familiar. We represented almost all states in the union, and every religion and socio-economic group in the country.

I took in the scene around me. The air held a hint of anxiety about what lay ahead. Within a few short hours, many of these new faces would be as familiar as the ten fellow Loretto Heights girls also destined for Austria.

We were the largest school contingent but my collegiate boundaries quickly expanded to encompass my fiery, fearless traveling companions: Nick, a short intense and outspoken Italian; Bob, a tall, stoic blue-eyed German who attended LaSalle College in Pennsylvania; Bruce, a medium-built handsome Anglo-Saxon Protestant attending the University of Washington; Judy, a

southern bell to the tips of her toes with a drawl you could slice
with a knife, from the University of Georgia; Cassandra (Nan), an
easy-going slender brunette from UCLA with undeniable
California-girl aura; worldly and mischievous Suzie from Salem
College in Winston-Salem, North Carolina; Marna, a classic blond
from the straight-laced College of St Teresa in Winona, Minnesota
whose helpless blue-eyed gaze attracted men like bees to honey
and who looked like a young sleek filly at the starting gate, ready
for a year of unrestrained freedom. The ship slipped away, and we
began the ancient dance and sway of introductions.

The IES headquartered in Chicago, conducted accredited
programs in several European cities. Students who had no
previous language skills (in our case, German) were invited to live
abroad in the home of a family in the country where they would
study. A full curriculum of accredited courses was offered and we
would be taught in English in the center of Vienna.

As we became proficient in German, a required course, it
was anticipated we could take other classes at the University of
Vienna campus. Living as part of an Austrian family helped each of
us quickly grasp language basics and local dialects. A lot depended
on individual affinities for learning a foreign language. My
"affinity" ranked bottom rung, but I worked hard, and a few beers
or glasses of new wine easily facilitated my German.

At that time, American students were welcomed with
open arms in Europe. The US exchange rate remained steady at
four to one. My parents covered the full cost of my year abroad
for less than a year at Loretto Heights, including travel to and
from Oregon.

The Statendam landed in Southampton on August 31,
1962, after seven luxurious days of cruising the Atlantic. This time
allowed the IESers, as we were called, to scope each other out
and determine a good roommate for the year. We ate delicious,
memorable food like a dessert named "The Flaming Baked
Alaska." I can still see the contingent of handsome, waist-coated
waiters swish into the hushed and darkened dining room carrying

high those flaming desserts on silver trays. My, oh my. Enjoying the evening nightclub acts, drinking and dancing the nights away made for an unforgettable cruise.

Landing, we wobbled on sea legs to our assigned buses, which took us via ferry and then overland to Vienna. Mr. Mowatt, a tall, raven-haired, gregarious gentleman, served as our tour bus director. He also taught classes for IES in Vienna. Mr. Mowatt's voice boomed through the bus, pointing out sights, maintaining a humorous running commentary on the highs and lows of European culture and history. For three weeks we would tour England, Belgium, France, Germany and then Austria, arriving in Vienna with a week to orient ourselves before classes began.

Mr. Mowatt was probably in his late twenties or early thirties, and I remember him in his long, navy blue, wool, overcoat set off by a dashing red scarf flipped over his shoulder. The scarf floated as he charged about, herding us hither and yon. All the IES girls had a crush on him. I recall one particularly brisk evening as I ran to catch the bus; Mr. Mowatt stood at the door, calling in heavily accented English,

"Come on Pat, you're holding us up."

"I'm coming as fast as I ... " Whoosh, I found myself enveloped in that huge wool coat, pressed tight against Mr. Mowatt's hard chest. I inhaled his musky scent, and I tried to catch my breath.

"Are you okay Liebchen?" he asked. Startled by the endearment, I could only nod and, weak-kneed, climb aboard the bus.

On the way to Brussels to hear lectures about the Common Market, our travels took us to Brugge, Belgium, the city of delicate handmade lace. Everywhere we went, IES provided educational and cultural opportunities. The students made sure to turn each stop into fun. On our way to Paris, our bus blew a tire, requiring all the buses to stop. We poured out in a frenzy of hugs, kisses and laughter and settled in to wait for the repair. Cards came out and practical jokes flourished, the monotony of the road alleviated.

Breezing through France and Germany en route to Austria, we felt awestruck by the diverse cultures, languages, food, customs, and lifestyles. Every country seemed to have its own unique toilet system: In Paris, I witnessed no modesty, pissiors right on street corners. Men entered and stood in a circle to do their business. Onlookers could easily observe. In a hotel room, I encountered my first bidet, which made for some interesting conversation and jokes. In Hungary, Greece, and Spain, a hole in the floor sufficed. On Greek ships, a hole extending over the sea made do. Newspaper, catalogue sheets, or rough brown paper, a real adjustment for our tender bottoms, replaced toilet paper. Meanwhile, in Germany and Austria, every public bathroom had an attendant waiting to be tipped.

Although I had fun absorbing unique customs and more's, the political happenings of this time were not entirely lost on me. While I was in Germany from 1962 to 1963, the German Democratic Republic constructed the Berlin Wall, completely cutting off East Berlin and East Germany from the West. Concurrently, Maureen had followed in Ellen's footsteps after college graduation and accepted a position with the Central Intelligence Agency, or CIA, as her best chance of traveling internationally and being posted overseas. While stationed in Berlin, she met and married a fellow operations officer, Dick. I got permission from IES to detour from Cologne, Germany, and visit the newlyweds in Berlin, then rejoin the IES bus caravan in Munich. It was exciting to meet tall, blue-eyed Dick, and he welcomed me warmly. Seeing Maureen again after being apart for a couple of years felt like reconnecting a lost limb. We grew close, and I marveled at the exciting life they lived.

I was fortunate that Dick helped me to see the import of the Wall and understand its history. He took me on my own private tour of the Wall. We drove around in his sexy white sports car with the black convertible top down so we could soak in the

71

warmth of September. Dick explained that throughout the 1950s and into the early 1960s, thousands of people from East Berlin crossed over into West Berlin to reunite with their families and escape Communist repression. In an effort to stop that outflow, on the night of August 12, 1961, the government of East Germany began to seal off all points of entrance into West Berlin by stringing barbed wire and posting sentries. In the days and weeks to come, construction of a concrete block wall began, as well as sentry towers and minefields. The U.S. government responded angrily. Commanders of American troops in West Berlin even made plans to bulldoze the Wall, but they gave up when the Soviets moved armored units into position to protect it. The West German government grew furious with America's lack of action, but President Kennedy believed that "A wall is a hell of a lot better than a war."

Dick parked the car so we could climb up on the viewing platform. Dick related the background of the Wall as we stood looking into East Berlin. East German soldiers patrolled the wall, rifles at the ready. The surreal scene before us remains etched in my mind: deathly quiet, the streets gray, bleak, and still. The only visible humans were the alert soldiers brandishing weapons. Many East Germans had already lost their lives trying to escape by climbing over the Wall (or by tunneling under). A terrified feeling gripped me as I took in that no man's land, and felt sympathy for all those trapped in East Germany.

My visit to Berlin went all too quickly, and soon I flew to Munich to rejoin the IES tour. Our journey culminated with the buses driving into Vienna early in the evening on September 17th. The city glowed in the twilight as the last of the day's sunbeams shimmered off the spire of St. Stephensdom, the famous cathedral in city center. During World War II, this symbol and centerpiece of Vienna was spared from intentional destruction at the hands of retreating German forces after a German Captain disregarded orders from the City Commandant to, "fire a hundred shells and leave it in debris and ashes."

As we drew closer and closer I felt anticipation and excitement build in our bus, and a hush settled. The beautiful city, our home away from home, lay before us to be explored and experienced leisurely over the next months. We had arrived.

Our buses deposited us at the IES dining hall in Luegerplatz, the center of the city. We stretched and began the next phase of our adventure. Dinner was waiting for us and the meal initiated our introduction to Austrian customs and life. Charlie, a snappy IESer from Wake Forest College in Illinois, offered his perspective, "Did you notice that the frauleins serving our tables don't shave their legs or their pits?"

Feeling a bit embarrassed and protective of these women, I remarked, "Charlie, it's the European custom, not just Austrian."

"I know that Pat, but she's carrying that loaf of bread under her hairy armpit! It's gross! And you know these Austrians don't bathe very often."

"Well you'd best get over it, Charlie. We won't be bathing very often either, and I bet after a while you won't even notice."

"That's not likely to happen," he said derisively. Charlie was not the only male in our group who carried this opinion, and it seemed to make American coeds more appealing.

During our bus trip across Europe, Alice and I decided to room together. Alice was an attractive fellow Heights junior from a large farming operation in southern Illinois and had similar values to my own. We did not know each other well, but we agreed to make a go of it. After dinner we were driven from the IES dining hall in the first district to our host family in the fifth district, a distance of 20 minutes by car, 30 minutes by bus or strassenbahn, or a 45-minute walk. Vienna's districts are 23 named city sections and we IESers were assigned to districts mostly in the lower numbers, presumably because most of our activities were in the center of the city. Frau Willman, the IES dean of students, asked her son Freddie to drive us to Brauhausgasse, 70/11/5 (this reflects the house number and the district) where we were assigned to live for the year with our host, Frau Geiginger. Alice and I felt nervous and excited to meet our hausfrau and to see her home.

We arrived at almost dark, noting the gray, drab exterior of the building. The street looked somber and unadorned, no trees or scrubs to soften the austere landscape.

On the drive to the apartment, Freddie told us Frau Geiginger had been widowed during World War II, and she managed by renting out her apartment to IES. She also took in some sewing and was a friend of our dean of students, who had recruited her. Other than that, we knew very little about her.

Freddie helped with our bags, and we entered through a heavy wooden door toward a stairway. "You're on the second floor" he said and nodded upwards. We circled up the concrete steps along dreary, plain walls. As we approached the second-floor landing, we could hear a door open. There at the top, smiling broadly, stood a middle-aged woman of small but plump stature, greeting us with open arms. "Kommen sie, Liebchen. Willkomen," she said with a heartiness that, in hindsight, rang false.

"Danka Schoen, Frau Geiginger," we chorused. That was the extent of intelligible conversation. Frau Geiginger spoke very little English, matching our limited German. She tried to make us feel welcome in her small apartment, speaking rapidly in Viennese dialect, but that proved even harder to understand.

Frau Geiginger's apartment included a small bathroom with a tub; a separate water closet (toilet); a Pullman kitchen—long and narrow, and her living quarters. Within the later were her bed, a few comfortable chairs, a dining room and the room Alice and I called home. Our room was cozy with two single beds draped in federdeckes (feather comforters, essential for warmth because there was no heat at night), a round oak dining table with two chairs, and two schranks (free-standing closets with drawers.)

There was no pleasing Frau Geiginger. Her attitude proved negative about almost everything we did. The list grew daily: we used too much toilet paper, too much hot water for our weekly bath, ate too many siemmels (delicious hard-crusted breakfast rolls, fresh from the bakery each morning) or wasted them along with the jam and butter … and on and on it went. None of the other kids seemed to have hausfrau issues and their host families enjoyed having American students in their homes. Alice and I believed Frau Geiginger actually resented American students as an imposition, even though they provided her with a much-needed income. Despite living with her for nearly a year we never became close or learned much more about her.

Classes began October 8th, and English-speaking instructors taught all of mine. Mr. Mowatt headed the philosophy department, and I took my logic class from him. Besides being able to gaze at Mr. Mowatt three times a week, I took advantage of other benefits afforded to IES students. Vienna is known for its beautiful opera house, and students were able to get stehplatz (standing room) for the performances for one shilling (about four cents). I knew nothing about opera or classical music, but I learned quickly by taking advantage of student rates. I saw Madame Butterfly, Cosi Fan Tutte, Carmen, Der Fledermaus, and Oedipus Rex, among others. The costuming and sets were beautiful, the singers extravagantly melodious, and the stories, acted out with voice and gestures, were enchanting.

A celebration not to be missed was the Munich October Fest. Twelve of us rented a Volkswagen bus—five girls and seven boys: Three of the boys were tall and gregarious: Kevin, also an Oregonian attending the University of Portland; Jeff from Colgate University; and Russ from the University of Southern California. Blond and lanky Mary Ann and her roommate, Vicki, both from Loretto Heights; Dan, very Italian and Catholic, from Holy Cross College; Gordy, a tall, dark-haired, quiet guy from the University of Wisconsin; worldly Nan from California; Alice; Nick; Charlie and, finally, me made up the dirty dozen.

We left Vienna at 8 p.m. on a Friday, and arrived at the outskirts of Munich at 3 a.m., parked, and tried to get some zzzz's. Twelve individuals in a nine-seater bus, does not for sleeping make; there was too much laughing, joking, farting and carrying on. Pulling into town, we found rooms at the International House, ate some food, actually slept, and then prepared for a night at the fest.

Beer houses the size of football stadiums covered the Munich fair grounds. Um-pa-pa music and German beer-drinking songs rang joyously throughout the tents. Everyone was gemutlich, (very, very happy.) They joined arms and swayed back and forth, singing at the tops of their lungs. The local folks, dressed in Tyrolean lederhosen and dirndls, were very serious about having a good time. We joined right in, and beer flowed like a river.

At one point I was hoisted up on our table to dance. I merrily accommodated, doing a twist to whatever was playing. From that vantage point, I saw the entire tented Hofbrauhaus with hundreds of people singing, drinking, and swaying. The payoff for dancing on "dem tisch" was that all the surrounding Germans bought my beer for the rest of the night. We ugly Americans managed to make off with 50 German beer steins tucked in shirts, coats and purses all stamped with the HB insignia for Hofbrauhaus. I claimed one mug, and today it rests on my mantle, bringing to mind fun and memorable times of my youth.

On a more serious note, October 1962 brought the Cuban Missile Crisis. Even though we were thousands of miles away, we felt the tension and worried about the danger our families and country faced. The news reported that the leaders of the United States and the Soviet Union were engaged in a tense, 13-day political and military standoff over the installation of nuclear-armed Soviet missiles on Cuba, just 90 miles from U.S. shores.

In a TV address on October 22, 1962, President Kennedy notified Americans about the presence of the missiles, explained his decision to enact a naval blockade around Cuba and made it clear the United States was prepared to use military force if necessary to neutralize this perceived threat to national security. Disaster was avoided when the United States accepted Soviet leader Nikita Khrushchev's offer to remove the Cuban missiles in exchange for an American promise not to invade Cuba.

Meanwhile we acclimated ourselves to the European school system which, at the college level, differed from our semester or quarter arrangement in the States. For example, it was not hard to adjust to the number of holidays. There were no classes on saints' days and it seemed we honored one every other week. Two weeks off at Christmas, and the whole month of February off as a semester break. Spring break meant three weeks for a bus trip throughout Italy, and we celebrated Easter in Rome.

While in Vienna what we did or did not do with our free time was left completely up to us. We could study, familiarize ourselves with the Viennese culture, travel, or drink ourselves silly on delicious beer or semi fermented new wine made from the season's first grape harvest and only available in autumn. There were no micromanagers to keep tabs. Managing this independence presented a thrilling challenge.

Not everyone in Europe owned a car. Fuel, even in 1962, proved pricey. Bicycles and motor scooters were the preferred mode of transportation. Unless all 100 of us IESers were transported somewhere by bus for pre-planned excursions, we hitchhiked. On any given weekend, we could cross borders by hitchhiking and return in time for classes Monday morning. In 1962-63, this was a very accepted practice, especially for students. Americans were welcomed. As long as we paired up, it was considered a safe way to travel.

During our semester break in February, five of us girls decided to take the train to Greece and hitchhike throughout the country. Our gang included Nan, Marna, Alice, Susie, and me. We allowed ourselves one-dollar-a-day spending money and often didn't even spend that, thanks to the generosity of the Greek people. We each traveled with one rucksack holding one black skirt, one black sweater, boots, tennis shoes, heels, three blouses, one pair of tights, one trench coat, three sets of bras and panties, one pair of cutoffs, a sweatshirt, one flannel shirt, one set of PJs, and toiletries.

One day, Nan and I teamed up to travel north through the Greek mountains. We caught a ride right away with a delightful man who took us to his simple, rustic farmhouse where we celebrated his wife's birthday. They wanted us to stay over so they could practice their English, but we were meeting friends in Delphi and needed to press on.

That afternoon, Nan and I stood on a very deserted road for what seemed like a long time. We were in the middle of the mountains, rucksacks thrown over our shoulders, when a lone car came along. Two men—one was a sailor, and both looked disheveled with rumpled clothing and oozing the pungent smell of bodies in need of a wash—slowed their car. Neither could speak anything but Greek. Nan, a wiz at languages, made them understand we needed a ride to Delphi.

"Okay Delphi!" exclaimed the sailor, the more gregarious of the two. He signaled us into the back seat. They drove fast, radio blaring, puffing smelly cigarettes, passing bread and coffee to us. The countryside appeared bleak, with little traffic and sparse population.

After an hour, they stopped at a dirty roadside shack, gesturing that we would eat. A small fire blazed in a corner of the shack and one dirty table made of two board planks, two chairs, and some log stumps made up the dining area. The proprietor, swathed in a grease stained apron, welcomed us with gestures to sit. Nan and I realized the potential danger, being stuck in the middle of nowhere. The men ordered chicken, which the proprietor caught from a handful running about the establishment. She hacked it to shreds, passed it over the open flames, and plopped it on the table along with tasteless, grainy pudding and wine. Our driver and the sailor were very jovial and continued drinking.

We returned to the car, and the sailor tried to get in the back seat with me. The mood had shifted. Nan managed to get into the back instead, and we drove on, the men propositioning. The driver, a big, muscular guy, watched me in his rearview mirror. His intense black eyes gleamed, and a salacious grin spread across his pocked, whiskery face. He had black, grimy teeth. All the while he dragged on his smelly cigarette, spewing blue smoke. The sailor gestured to himself, thumping proudly on his grease-stained chest, then at me, then to the driver, and then Nan, saying the only English he knew: "1, 2, 3, 4."

We responded, laughing in unison, trying to keep things light, "5, 6, 7, 8." The sailor shook his head furiously and gestured vigorously. His face became shiny and red with the effort. Himself—1. Me—2. The driver—3. Nan—4. We kept responding, "5, 6, 7, 8," feigning ignorance of his intentions. We were frightened out of our wits, knowing we could be easily overpowered. Our arsenal included only a nail file. After an hour of this, the men grew angry at our stupidity. With relief, Nan and I noticed lights ahead and knew Delphi was within reach.

"Pay," blurted the driver. He came to a jerky stop just outside the Delphi city limits. "No 1, 2, 3, 4! You pay 50 Drachmas!" Shaking, we made a big show of digging around in our rucksacks and pulled out 22 Drachmas and 75 cents.

"That's it. It's all we have," exclaimed Nan, as she pushed me out the door "No more." To me, she said, "Move it, Pat—fast." We ran, putting distance between them and us and thanking God we'd arrived unscathed. We headed for the youth hostel and the security of our friends.

The close encounter remained the only one of its kind in our travels throughout the whole European continent. In hindsight, I can plainly see that the outcome might have been horribly different. We both learned a lesson that, if shared with our parents, would have had us heading home on the next plane.

You learn a lot about a person under these circumstances: the good, the bad, and the ugly. Nan and I decided to room together during the IES Easter trip to Italy, and if that worked out, we would travel together all summer.

My most vivid memory of Italy is Easter Sunday morning at St. Peter's Square in Rome, waiting for Pope John XXIII to appear on his balcony. Thousands filled the square in the Vatican City, and we secured a spot next to the gray steel barricades directly below the Pope's balcony. IESers Jim, Jeff, and John joined Nan and me as we waited. A hush descended. Looking up, we saw the doors to the balcony open. The Pope appeared in his pristine white robe and cap, and thousands pushed forward as one, shoving us into the barricades. Pope John raised his arm to give his Easter blessing and the crowd surged again, flattening us. Being of a small body build and somewhat claustrophobic, I offered little resistance to the crowd and remember feeling terrified that I might lose footing and be trampled to an ink spot. Jeff hollered, "Pat, here, hold on to me and John!" Each took one of my arms and blocked me with their bodies from the barricade and the crowd.

The Pope's Easter blessing ended and the crowd eased. I hugged the boys, exclaiming, "John, Jeff, you saved my life! I don't know how to thank you. That really scared me! I hate to think what might've happened if you hadn't been here. Let's go have a glass of wine."

I wasn't the only one of our group shaken more by the power of the crowd than the spiritual supremacy of the Pope. We all had waited our whole lives to see and hear him. It's sad to realize now that my lasting memory of that event is the terror of the crowd.

Nan and I began making serious plans for our summer, calling us Higgins, Horton & Company. Like our trip to Greece, we limited what clothes we took in our rucksacks. For the first leg of our journey, we planned to hitchhike from Vienna through Switzerland, down to Barcelona, and then fly to the island of Majorca. We had a total of six summer weeks, with plans to leave Vienna on June 26th after our final exams. Our ambitious itinerary would ultimately take us all the way to Denmark and then to Rotterdam to catch a returning ship to America.

Leaving Vienna was tearfully painful. We had all become so close over the past year, and now we were going our separate ways. Many of us were following the same travel route and hoped to run into each other. I will always remember those magical final weeks of spring in Vienna. Dull, gray, winter skies of the worst winter in Vienna's history gave way to the full flush of a warm and colorful spring, fragrances drifting in the air. Bright grass adorned the city's many parks, perfect places to lull around discussing the future of the world and our places in it—and how we might make it better. Living arrangements with the curmudgeonly Frau Geiginger didn't seem quite so grim, and the advent of spring enabled us to get outdoors and roam the city. Intuitively, I knew this European experience changed me. I saw the world with new eyes and was now ready to seek out the likenesses in people of different cultures rather than being distracted by their differences.

Parting was especially difficult for another reason as well. John was tall, green-eyed, and intense, and we discovered each other in those last few short weeks, beginning a lovely romance. We parted much too soon. John would travel across Europe with Jeff that summer, then return to the States to finish college—John to Georgetown University, and Jeff to New York University. They both lived in or near New York City and had been acquainted prior to their junior year abroad. John invited me to meet his family at their Long Island home once we were Stateside.

My one memory of that interlude, in the states, is driving the turnpike with John at the wheel and his Mom beside me in the front seat. They were taking me back to the city to meet my Aunt Charlotte. Traffic was very heavy, and his mom turned to me and said, "Pat, John's going to show you how we deal with people who climb up the back of you when you're on the turnpike in three lanes of traffic like this. OK, John, do it!" I turned around to see a car inches from our back bumper just as John turned on his lights. The guy riding our tail thought John had braked. Honks resounded as we streamed away from the angry tailgater, teaching me a lesson in effectively dealing with jerks.

John and I followed different paths in life that didn't permit us to meet up again. I wonder now if he still has that slow, sexy grin that lit his eyes as it slid across his slender face or, that unruly shock of black hair spilling over his forehead. I had let myself dream a little about a life with John, but like a shipboard romance, it fizzled once our feet were planted back on U.S. soil.

In retrospect that European summer's impressions include generous local people in every country; heavy rucksacks filled with dirty clothes; succulent strawberry pie in the Zurich train station; bedbugs in the youth hostels of Barcelona; pathetically standing in the pouring rain thumbing for rides; sick with colds; tired and broke; the hot Majorcan sun returning us to health; lovely art, museums, and stunning architecture everywhere; dazzling countryside; and the fierce and loving friendships that grew between fellow IESers. I see these things as pinpoints of light across a canvas of heartfelt memories alive with emotion. After experiencing such freedom and growth in so few months I privately wondered about home: would anyone notice the change in me?

By mid-August, the Rotterdam steamed into Verrazano Narrows at the outer edges of New York harbor, returning me to my country. I immediately longed for the freedom and independence Europe had offered. Instead, I faced a structured, conservative year at Marylhurst College. I had made the decision not to return to Loretto Heights midway through my European experience. I knew I would be filled to the brim with rules and expectations, but it would be a big cost savings to my parents. Additionally, my two sisters had graduated from Marylhurst and the Holy Name nuns had preconceived ideas about Higgins girls. I wasn't sure if that would work for or against me. Switching schools meant I would miss not only the IESers, but also my Heights friends, a decision I hoped I would not regret as our ship brought us ever closer to the dock.

As the Statue of Liberty unveiled herself from the morning mist, my heart leapt at her significance to all those who came fleeing tyranny and oppression. They sought freedom and democracy, and our country welcomed them. The Europeans had welcomed me in return. They proclaimed passionately, "You are the greatest country in the world, the most powerful. You help all of us and stand for liberty and peace."

Tears trickled down my cheeks, and my vision blurred as I took in this great lady's stature. My chest spilled over with gratitude for the opportunities given, the sacrifices made, that I might have that year to test my wings and broaden my horizons, to prepare for the challenges that lay ahead.

Pitchfork

Senior year of college, surprisingly, afforded a rich and memorable time with my parents. I convinced myself the reason for attending Marylhurst for my last year was financial, saving Mom and Dad a lot of money. I would also be only an hour from home. Both were true. However, the real motivation underlying the decision to transfer colleges lay in the fact that Loretto Heights College required seniors to take oral exams in order to graduate. This prospect paralyzed me. I had never been one to raise my hand in class and facing oral exams in my history class at IES had terrified me, so I created a life-changing smoke screen to avoid facing those exams. Who knew? No one, and it took many years before I allowed myself to face up to this truth.

Mom and Dad came to campus at least once a week with money to spare for dinner out, lunch, shopping, or to see a movie. Several times, Mom came alone to spend the weekend with me. I didn't have a roommate in my dorm room, and time away from Dad gave Mom a mini vacation.

On one such occasion, we returned to campus from a day of shopping and dinner in Portland. She and I were nestled in our beds in pajamas when she shared a particularly humorous, but sad story with me. Her eyes danced across the space between our twin beds, eager with a secret. She sat up straight, squared her shoulders and took a steading breath.

"Pat, I'd had it," she said. "I'm not sure exactly what tipped me over the edge, but you should've seen it. Dad was in the kitchen. He was going out to the orchard, and he made one of those cutting remarks."

I nodded. She didn't have to tell me what Dad had said. I could have guessed any number of insults and understood the gist.

"I followed your Dad out the back door and screamed, 'You bastard, Joe! I've enough of your sarcasm!'"

At this my eyes widened. Years later, when I studied graphoanalysis (the study of handwriting), I learned that sarcasm is first and foremost a weapon, employed in either defense or offense. Mom's story made me both angry with our Dad's past hurts and proud that she finally stood up to him.

"Pat, without knowing quite how, there's the pitchfork in my hand … it seemed to take on a life of it's own as I angled it toward Dad. He started backing up … slowly at first. Then he was on the back lawn turning away … me sprinting with the pitchfork extended … and Pat, he actually started running! So I chased him around the clothes line screaming at him all the way!" At this point Mom was doubled over in laughter at the telling. I laughed in disbelief at the scene in my mind's eye.

I knew that Dad used sarcasm with extreme skill, leaving his audience laughing at the expense of his victim. In Mom's case, he knew how to pierce her heart or undermine her keen mind. He'd render her weakened and unable to find her bearings. Perhaps he wanted to crush her spirit. He even laughed behind his hand when Mom's crystal blue eyes sparked with tears or anger as she fought to maintain her dignity.

"Good for you Mom! So then what happened?"

"I actually pinned him. I had the pitchfork at his chest. I told him never to talk to me or treat me that way again. Oh, Pat! It was delicious. He actually looked scared, and you know I was mad enough to run him through, and I think he knew it."

"It must've felt really good to stand up to him like that, Mom," I said, going to her and giving her a hug.

"Yes," Mom said, "Yes, it did."

I proudly saw myself as one who faced challenges, but I recognized the cowardice in my decision to change colleges when I heard my Mother speaking up for herself from her heart— pitchfork in hand! This shamed me. I was an avoider. Rather than admit to the truth of a situation, I turned my back. Perhaps even worse when given the chance, I wouldn't know what to say.

Sadly, I never saw any lasting results from Mom's brave attack and they settled back into their old patterns. It gave me cause to observe that the apple doesn't fall from the tree. An apt student of my father, from a young age, I could spar and take pride in outdoing an opponent. It took wit and intelligence to deliver a killing blow, quickly deciphering when and what would shred the recipient. Seeing only victory, and not understanding the damage I inflicted. Pride bloomed while "performing" in front of my dad. Making him laugh out loud, felt as good as catching the brass ring on a merry-go-round.

Classmates and friends I entertained with sarcastic wit at the expense of others. The textbook description says, "those who use it (sarcasm) do so to defend themselves in ego-threatening situations, give vent to frustrated feelings, or provide expression for malicious desires." I describe it as one of the most detrimental traits a person can possess because I've seen it in action. Sarcasm erects barriers between people, forestalls conversation, and artificially enhances the intellectual self-image and ego of the one delivering the barb. Those barriers provided the perfect concealment for things closely held.

The Higgins family kept secrets. Keeping acquaintances and friends at a safe distance proved an effective ploy. At that stage, I didn't understand what the Higgins secrets were, just that no one could get close enough to discover what lay behind Dad's intrigue. We were taught not to talk about family actions to anyone. Those admonitions wreaked havoc on friendships. Mom called me "Judy-Friendly" because I tended to be gregarious and liked meeting and talking with people. Inevitably, as a budding relationship began to grow and confidences were exchanged, I pulled back in the only way I knew how. Sarcastic wit whittled most new friends to sawdust, destroying what might otherwise have been a long and rewarding relationship.

After an independent year in Europe with both male and female friends, Marylhurst proved more challenging than anticipated. I was familiar with its setting: an all women's enclave where friendships had solidified over three years. My new college mates were not particularly receptive to expanding their intimate circles. The Sisters of the Holy Names of Jesus and Mary ran a conservative and tight ship. Their predecessors came from Quebec in 1893 to found Marylhurst, the first liberal arts college serving the educational needs of Pacific Northwest women. Their reputation for excellence stood the test of time, but I found myself ill suited to the strongly structured environment. My previous exposure to the much more liberal Lorentine nuns made Holy Name rigidity taxing to my young spirit.

A secretarial job working for the Dean of Students and avidly pursuing my studies, helped resign myself to a year of stifling restrictions, conservative thinking, an abundance of rules, and **no** men. It did not take long to realize that the good dean, Sister Mary Margaret, had hired me to keep me under her thumb. To her way of thinking, my year in Europe might make me susceptible to negatively influencing the other girls.

The positive results of this torture chamber were that, with effort, I made a few friends among my classmates. I earned a spot on the dean's list both semesters, and the CIA recruiter, Mr. Tom Culhane came calling. Marylhurst was on his list of colleges for potential CIA candidates. He'd successfully recruited Ellen and Maureen during their senior years and he convinced my California IES travel companion, Nan to consider joining the Agency's ranks and me.

What would life be like as a spy? In 1964, women with college degrees mostly became teachers or nurses. Those who didn't generally started as clerks or clerk-typists to get their foot in the door. My sisters never revealed what they actually did on their CIA assignments. James Bond's *Goldfinger* movie was my model. Watching the female lead vamp about, seducing foreign spies. Naive about the cloak-and-dagger life, but choosing a career not to be shared with others fit into my model of secrecy in which I had grown up, it was thrilling.

President Kennedy created the Peace Corps before his untimely death in 1963, and I felt moved by the prospect of "doing good." The Peace Corps accepted me to teach English in Senegal, a small East African country. However, Mr. Culhane worked his CIA charm, convincing me I was an ideal candidate for a life of intrigue. I grew so starry-eyed that I cannot recall my offering even a flimsy argument as to why I might not be an ideal candidate. Perhaps it was thought that "good" Catholic girls were doctrinally brainwashed, easily malleable as spies. For me, the real hook seemed clear: travel abroad. Both Ellen and Maureen were stationed overseas with the Agency by that time, having started out the same way, and both had met and married Agency operatives.

Mr. Culhane explained that I would start as a clerk-typist, but my college education would open the door for rapid progress, including overseas assignments. That sounded much more intriguing than teaching English in a third-world country. After talking with Nan, she agreed to toss her name into the hat. Mr. Culhane was doubly pleased.

Standing at the juncture of graduation and a career, I thought back to the family house on Davis Road. It sat back off the road, Venetian blinds always drawn. Dad liked to make people wonder. So far, all four siblings had kept the secret about Dad's name change from Loschiavo to Higgins. There were other secrets, too, like Mom's half-brother, still in Germany, conceived out of wedlock. When I announced my decision to join the CIA, Dad seemed more excited by that than by anything else I'd done in my twenty-two years. He loved the mystery associated with the CIA and beamed with pride as I crossed the Marylhurst graduation stage to receive my diploma. I, on the other hand, was chagrined that this should be the focus of Dad's pride. After all, I had achieved honor roll status. Since first grade I could not remember Dad ever demonstrating satisfaction with my grades. They were never good enough. Now they were, and the bittersweet truth was that it didn't seem to matter.

Go East Young Woman, Go East

"WhoooWhooooo," the Union Pacific train wailed as it chugged south along the Oregon coast making its way to Oakland. On this defining day in June 1964, I was filled with promise. I settled in a window seat, mesmerized. Dense wooded mountains and a jagged seacoast streamed by. The clackity-clack of train wheels simultaneously whisked me closer to my destination and farther from my roots near Hood River. I now had full responsibility for myself—food, clothes, shelter and whatever else it took to make my way. There was No going back.

A Higgins girl didn't go back, no matter what lay ahead. Exhilarated and downright scared, my stomach back flipped as we chugged closer and closer, farther and farther, feeling like I was falling down Alice's rabbit hole. By the time the train pulled into the Oakland terminal, I'd talked myself into quite a tizzy. Seeing Nan pierced the gloom.

Nan and I hauled my bags over the front steps of her home, then up to her bright spacious bedroom in the Horton home. We sat on the bedroom's window seat, backlit by three bay windows. A light breeze rippled the gauzy curtains. Nan looked tentative. "Pat, my Mom's not here. But I've to go see her." Nan paused as I quickly processed the information. "Will you go with me?"

"Sure," I said. "But when? Where's she?" Excited to be in California for the first time, I wasn't ready to get back in the car for an errand. Nan searched the kitchen, pulling ingredients from the fridge. She moved deftly, apparently a practiced cook, but a look of concern caught my attention.

"We can go after dinner," Nan said. She squatted down and opened a drawer in the bottom of the fridge. "Here." She handed me a large, prickly, green vegetable. Whatever worry had surfaced moments before had passed. She looked the picture of a glowing young woman—the closest friend I had in years.

"Ever eaten artichokes?" she asked.

"Nope, sure haven't."

"I'll show you how it's done." Nan stood to close the refrigerator door. She smiled at me, her mother forgotten. "California style."

"I'm willing to try," I said, "but what about these thorns?"

Nan laughed, tossing her long black hair over her shoulders. I loved the way she always seemed so comfortable with herself. Perhaps I was wrong to worry about Nan's mother. Everything would turn out fine. This was California, after all, an Oregon-raised farm-bred ready-for-more girl's dream come true. If it meant a thorn or two here and there, I could take it.

Nan's younger sister Jett and her little brother Teddy joined us for dinner. Their Dad was working late on a real estate deal, and I would meet him tomorrow. Nan was a surprisingly good cook. She prepared a saucy chicken dish to go with the artichokes and a big tossed salad. I fell in love with artichokes that day, scraping my teeth along the stiff leaves after dipping them in mayonnaise. Then, there lay the prize, the delicious heart revealed only after all the outside leaves were eaten and the hairy choke removed. Foodie heaven. I did think it bizarre that the family dog got to lick all the plates at the table, but that proved just the beginning of what I learned in that California world of Hortons.

Dinner over, dishes licked (and, as I noticed with relief, put in the dishwasher), Nan spoke up.

"Okay, Pat let's go see my Mom."

"Where exactly is she, Nan?"

"She's in the hospital," Nan replied. We got into her car, and I looked at Nan, arching a black expectant eyebrow. She reluctantly went on, refusing my gaze. "Mom had a bad fall and has been in the hospital for about a week." Her tone indicated the discussion was closed. "Let's go … and get it over with." She flipped the car radio channels to her favorite Beethoven sonata and turned it up loud.

As Nan drove along the tree lined streets, her hands clenched the wheel her brow furrowed in concentration. I thought Nan a classic beauty with her angular nose, high cheekbones, and silky black hair framing her face. Self-possessed, smart, and fun to be with, I realized that even though we spent the better part of a year traveling through Europe, Nan hadn't spoken much about her parents. Taken aback by her reluctant attitude, I grew nervous about what lay ahead. Her elusiveness would prove to be a good quality for a spy.

We walked down the quiet corridor of an obviously exclusive private hospital. Pausing at the door to one of the rooms, Nan took a deep breath. She squared her shoulders and slowly opened the door.

"Hi, Mom. How're you doing today?" she asked.

I took in the scene before me. There lay a diminutive woman, dark brown hair surrounding her badly battered face. Her arms were sheathed in purple, green, and orange bruises, her hands clutching frantically at her covers. I tried very hard to conceal my shock. I was dismayed and also angered at Nan for giving me no clue as to what was going on with her mother, and our stilted visit proved no more enlightening. We drove out of the hospital parking lot and I asked quietly, "Nan, what happened?"

"She took a really bad fall about a week ago—oh, all right, Pat," Nan said. Her face reddened. "You might as well know. Mom's an alcoholic. She got so drunk she fell down the stairs at home, broke her glass, and got cut up with that too. This's been going on for a long time, and it's not the first time she's ended up in the hospital."

"Nan, those bruises on her face and neck …?"

"Yeah, well that's what happened."

I could only offer sympathy and an ear if Nan needed one. Knowing it best to let this painful subject drop, we lapsed into making plans for our cross-country trip.

After a leisurely breakfast the next morning, we planned to head into San Francisco across the Golden Gate Bridge and Nan was going to show me the sights. But first, we stopped by her Dad's office. When we walked into Mr. Horton's office he was speaking on the phone.

"Yes, Mom, I know that. No, I don't think that's such a good idea," he said.

"But George, that's what I want to do and you need to help me, okay?" Her voice rang through on speakerphone.

"Mom you know I've a business to run ..."

Mr. Horton waved us in, signaling for us to take the chairs in front of his desk while he went on with this conversation. I had never seen a speakerphone in use before. His mother continued cajoling him while he signed letters and checks, never missing a beat. He responded occasionally, "Yes, Mom," "No Mom," "Ummmmhum." Finally he signed off: "Love you, Mom, see you for lunch tomorrow."

Mr. Horton unfolded behind his desk like the long green bean man in my childhood storybook. Tall, angular, and strikingly handsome, with a sprinkle of salt and pepper in his dark hair, he stood, and then walked around his imposing desk in an easy stride. Next came a warm, welcoming hug into the Horton family. The moment lodged in my mind because of its incongruity—the casual way he conducted his business as his wife lay tattered in the hospital. I could not mesh the pieces of this family puzzle in my mind and found it troubling. Nan's relationship with her Dad was amicably close and supportive, while she appeared dutiful and distant from her Mom. I knew when the time seemed right, Nan would reveal more. Perhaps I would disclose some of my own world, too. I knew that talking and sharing built and strengthened friendships, but I had scant examples to go on. We chatted about safe subjects like my home in Oregon and plans for our trip across the country.

For her college graduation, Nan's Dad gifted her with a brand new, fire-engine-red Chevrolet convertible, complete with a snow-white top. We were going to drive it across the whole United States! To add to the fun, Esso (now Exxon-Mobil) had just

launched its advertising campaign to "Put a Tiger in your Tank."
Copy for the ad read, "The tiger is seen as the king of the forest. It
epitomizes regality, supremacy strength, and energy. Don't you
like having the king empowering you as you speed down the
highway fast and free?" The ad depicted a lovable tiger cartoon
character, which was just catching on. We bought a tiger tail sold
by Esso and let it hang out of the gas tank, anxious to see what
mischief it caused on the open road. This advertising campaign
was one of the most successful in history, and *Time* magazine
found it worthy to proclaim 1964 as "The Year of the Tiger".

We packed our belongings in the car, gassed up at 27 cents
per gallon, said our goodbyes to the Horton family, and set off
with jaunty waves. Within minutes, we rolled the top down, the
wind in our hair and the sun on our faces, beginning our grand
adventure. Nan visibly relaxed with each advancing mile. Music
blared, and she coached and quizzed me on composers of her
favorite classical pieces. "Okay, Pat name this piece and who
composed it."

"Oh, Nan," I would groan, "I don't know." Even after a year
in Vienna, I couldn't remember one piece or tell one composer
from another. I liked what appealed to my ear, but beyond that I
was like a sieve with water, musically speaking.

When a popular song like "I Get Around" by the Beach
Boys, "Under the Boardwalk" by the Drifters or "A Hard Day's
Night" by the Beatles wafted across the airwaves, we belted out
the lyrics. Nan could carry a tune, but I sounded like a canary with
a seed stuck in its throat. We shared the driving and played
games, like seeing how many red, blue, black, or white cars we
could count. We also enjoyed identifying the makes of passing
cars. We laughed, giggled, and imagined the excitement of our
new jobs, entertaining visions of super spies.

The stir and excitement that our tiger tail inspired as we
sped along our route turned our minds toward the future. Truck
drivers honked and waved enthusiastically as we raced by in the

passing lane. Nan never revealed much more about her mom. For my part, I never let on how anxious I felt about what lay ahead.

After five eventful, fun filled but weary days, we arrived in Northern Virginia to stay with my sister, Ellen until we could find a place to live. We found a small, furnished townhouse on 34th street in the Georgetown section of Washington, D.C., exactly where we wanted to set up housekeeping. It was an easy bus commute to where we reported to the CIA on K Street for in-processing. The house stood at the end of a block, two stories high, appointed with white-washed brick, black shutters, and a red door with a brass door knocker. August was sweltering and humid but, in 1964, air-conditioning was not commonplace. We dressed for work in girdles, nylons, slips, suits, and heels, returning home a soggy perspiring mess at the end of the day.

The first Monday morning we were to report looms large in my memory. Nan seemed calm, not the least bit nervous. I felt like a bowl of Jello. We rose early to allow extra time to find a parking space, since we had decided to drive the first day to give us time to learn the bus schedules. The heat, already oppressive, compounded my apprehension.

After parking, we followed our written instructions to the K Street address and stood before a very nondescript, cream-colored door. It offered no indication of what lurked beyond. We walked up the narrow staircase to a large room with small desks. It looked like a college classroom. We took our seats, waiting to see what would happen next.

To get to this point we had completed detailed applications. We revealed everything we had done or thought about doing since we came into this world, and with whom. A six-month investigation assured, beyond any reasonable doubt, that we were who we claimed to be. CIA investigators talked and dug into every aspect of our pasts, including every place we ever lived and every relative in our lineage. Friends and neighbors were interviewed about our interests, characters, likes and dislikes. What more could there possibly be? A lot, it turned out.

The officer in charge of our induction stood at the front of the room dressed in a white short-sleeved shirt, blue tie, and navy pants. Looking calm in the heat of the room, he made it clear we weren't "in-the-door" until we passed a polygraph test, better known as a lie detector test, as well as typing speed and accuracy exams.

"We don't want you to be overly concerned, but this polygraph test is a critical part of your in-processing," he explained. "It'll be conducted at Langley Headquarters, and it enables us to weed out anyone unsuited to this line of work."

This was news to me. I quaked in my seat. The officer continued and we learned, for instance, that homosexuals were widely regarded as vulnerable to blackmail and, therefore, a strong security risk. This rationale prevailed in all Intelligence Agencies in the 1960s, and the country itself treated gays with prejudice and disdain. In the late 1990s, the CIA adopted a more inclusive attitude, even actively recruiting homosexuals.

We were discouraged from fraternizing with anyone outside the Agency, since we were not permitted to talk about our work except with coworkers. Ultimately, the polygraph test would determine a candidate's suitability for spy work.

"You're assigned to this K Street office until your top-secret clearances come through, and that can still take several weeks," the officer concluded. He paced to a halt at the front of the room, looked sternly at each of us and then dismissed the group.

As Nan and I drove back to our townhouse, I felt dirty and discouraged. "I'm really worried about that polygraph test," I said.

"Why? You'll breeze through. You're—pure as the driven snow!" She arched her fine, dark eyebrows at me. "I'm the one who should be worried, silly."

But I did have concerns tucked away, hardly pure as snow. My subconscious came to full attention. Dare I hope the CIA would clearly see that I did **not** have homosexual tendencies? That a junior assigned as my big sister stalked me freshman year

95

at Loretto Heights? That naive me was completely unaware that my safe world included such a predator, let alone what to do when ensnared in her clutches? I could not bring myself to discuss the fears with anyone, not even Nan, and I grew terrified that I would be disgraced.

Even though I met and became aware of a gay person for the first time in college, I hadn't any formulated concept, awareness, or prejudice of gays as a group. I didn't understand that to be gay might be an actual sexual orientation, let alone something that could prevent a person from being hired. Later, I would understand the larger social and political context. Fresh out of college and small town life, I could only fret about what it might mean for my career.

Days passed and I successfully scaled every other entrance hurdle with flying colors. But my polygraph test date drew nearer. I couldn't eat. Sleeping proved fitful, filled with frightening nightmares of my trying to explain to my parents why the CIA refused me. Sarcasm wouldn't work here—what could I possibly say? Avoidance wouldn't work either. Defenseless against the technology that could peek behind the facade, I tossed and turned every night that week, always coming up empty.

The fateful day dawned sunny but hazy, air as heavy as my heart. I dragged myself to the shower and painstakingly prepared for what lay ahead. The only approach was to put my best face forward, tell the truth, and let the rest take care of itself.

After getting myself down to K Street on the bus, I caught an unmarked shuttle to Langley, Virginia, a 45-minute ride to destiny; my first—and possibly last—visit to CIA Headquarters. The shuttle exited off Virginia's route 123 and traveled a half-mile to a heavily guarded gate. Butterflies took full flight in my stomach, my breath coming in shallow gasps and my skin clammy. I coached myself to breathe deeply. I knew I could do this … everything depended keeping a cool head. Even though they told us only the top five percent of the applicant population makes it into this place, I tried to convince myself not to be intimidated, but I remember thinking, "Dear God, I **am** intimidated and I need **Your** help on this one."

The shuttle pulled to a stop at the entrance to the bold, futuristic structure. I stepped into the majestic marble foyer and felt like a speck on a sleeve. I waited to be escorted to the interrogation room and sat for what seemed like an eternity. Finally, a receptionist called.

"Miss Higgins, this officer will escort you to your appointment now." I was so inwardly focused and frightened that I cannot remember much about the long walk, only that my legs barely supported me as we traversed a searingly bright, windowed corridor on the second floor. We turned down a dark hallway with glass-walled interrogation rooms on either side.

"Miss Higgins, please take a seat. Your polygraph exam will begin in just a few minutes," the officer said. I sat in the black leather chair taking deep breaths and viewing my surroundings. A single light illuminated the equipment and chair with a halo effect. Goose bumps rose on my arms. The room's temperature chilled and sterile from the air-conditioning, was an obvious perk of the new building. I noticed to my right and slightly behind my chair rested the metal polygraph machine and a stool for the operator. There was a graph-like machine as well with a pointy metal needle, I assumed to record my reactions to the questions. Suddenly the door swung open.

"Good morning, Pat ... may I call you Pat?" I looked up and saw a slender, cleanly shaved man wearing a crisp white shirt, navy tie, and perfectly pressed tan pants.

"Yes, that's fine." Anything, I thought, to relax this whole scene and get it over with.

"Good. I'm going to be the one administering your polygraph exam this morning. I want you to try and relax. There's nothing to worry about, and the whole thing should only take about 20 minutes." He had a quiet, soothing voice.

"Okay, but I am nervous," I admitted, my voice quivering.

"I understand," he said sympathetically. "You'll see, it'll be fine. I'm going to hook you up to this recording machine and then ask you some test questions so you can see how it's going to work. Then the actual test will begin." He placed a strap around my high middle, just under my breasts, and warned, "This test is specifically designed to detect whether or not you are telling the truth. So honesty is the best policy."

The questions began innocuously enough: "Is your name Pat? Did you grow up in Oregon?" Gradually they became more intense: "Have you ever been drunk? Do you often drink to excess?" All of the questions elicited a "yes" or "no" answer. The question I most feared reared its head: "Have you ever engaged in homosexual activity?" Out of the corner of my eye I saw the recording needles jump off the charts.

What should have taken 20 minutes stretched into a two-hour session of questions and pauses while I dripped with sweat and shook with chills. The examiner left the room to consult with his supervisor, only to return and begin again. It was a thoroughly draining experience, surely skewing the test results even more dramatically. Finally, the examiner sighed. "Pat we're done here for now. But we've made an appointment for you to see our agency psychiatrist. Let's get you unhooked and I'll escort you to his office."

"What do you mean, 'done for now?'" I asked. This was an experience I did not want to repeat.

"Our psychiatrist will decide if we need to continue the testing," he explained. "I've arranged for you to see him now." Things seemed to be going from bad to worse. I thought only crazy people needed to see psychiatrists. All right, one more hurdle...

The psychiatrist sat, mouse-like, behind a large steel desk, spectacles rested on the tip of his long nose, hair slicked back from his forehead. He peered at me with beady brown eyes, clearly interested, as he blatantly looked me up and down.

"Miss Higgins, please come in, and may I call you Pat?" His silky voice came at me smoothly, and I wasn't sure I could trust it.

"Yes, of course, please do," I replied. I realized that dressing with care that morning made an impact on this man. I determined to level the playing field and use his interest to my advantage. Intuitively, I knew the curtain had risen.

After a few banalities, he dove right into the matter. "Pat you've been through a lot in the last few hours. I want you to try and relax now so we can have a quiet chat. I just need to clarify a few things and help determine your suitability for working at the Agency. The area of concern is the relationship you had with your college big sister. Can you please tell me about that?"

This man, the first person to hear the whole story, held my future in his hands. I became very emotional in the telling. Tears of fear or regret, probably both, flowed as I gazed directly into his eyes with my imploring blue ones, black eyelashes batting away tears. Seeing my last tissue soggy with tears, he came around the desk, Kleenex box in hand

"There, there, Pat," he soothed. His other arm went around my shoulders in a comforting, yet suggestive gesture, almost a caress.

"Thank you," I croaked with a watery smile and I accepted the tissue. I wiped my eyes, keeping them averted, as he stood too close.

"Pat, I can clearly see you were victimized by this woman, and you were obviously inexperienced in the ways of the world." I sighed in relief as he returned to the other side of the desk. "The Agency must be very careful in its selection process. We have to make sure that our employees cannot be coerced or blackmailed by enemy agents because of something that happened in their past. Pat, now that you recognize and understand your own heterosexual orientation, I see this event during college as just a life experience we can put behind us. Do you agree?"

"Oh, yes sir, I do," I nodded reassured and mentally fist-punched the sky. Relief warmed me like a blanket.

"I see no reason why you won't enjoy a long and prosperous career with the Agency, Pat. I am recommending that your in-processing proceed without delay. It's been my pleasure meeting you today." He walked me to the door, arm around my shoulders, squeezing to assure I understood his interest.

Escorted through security and out the building entrance, I felt almost faint. I had done it. I'd saved my job and probably my reputation along with it. On the other hand, I was not proud of manipulating the psychiatrist with my dramatic, tearful telling.

As I stood on the white marble steps with the brilliant sun reflecting, I breathed a sigh of relief and began to imagine the exciting career of subterfuge that awaited. But within the crevices of joy remained a deep sense of loneliness, guilt and shame with its grip wrapped around a story that I could not share with family, friends or even fully during the polygraph test. At that moment, I tucked away those hauntings, but memories, especially bad ones, have a way of rising from the ashes, even if they take decades to surface again.

Undaunted

The CIA placed me undercover in the Directorate of Operations. When people asked where I worked, I'd respond with the Agency cover story, "I work for the Department of the Army." Then, I'd hope that my inquisitor would not delve too deeply with more questions. The CIA admonition that "Loose Lips Sink Ships" is truer than most might imagine.

The Directorate of Operations was another name for the clandestine services. Its structure was comprised of divisions representing sections of the world, such as the Far East division, the Europe division and the South America division.

I served for a year on the German desk at Langley, as a clerk-typist and then as an intelligence assistant before being assigned overseas to Cologne, Germany. It was difficult to make friends outside the Agency. Everything we did or said necessitated discretion, a seductive smile behind a flared fan.

A typical daily routine involved approaching the main gate designated on the highway sign as "BPR" a misnomer that stood for the Bureau of Public Roads. I flashed my picture badge, then drove through the gate and showed the ID again at the guarded doors of the building. The day's order of business was to dial the combination to my assigned safe and retrieve all the work stored the previous night. We left nothing on our desks at day's end. When my desk phone rang, I answered using a 4-digit extension, never my name or office designation. Phone conversations could be easily monitored. Guarding our speech to avoid revealing sensitive information was paramount. All discarded documents and trash I tore into small pieces and dropped in my "burn bag." This bag was similar to a brown grocery bag, only narrower, with large red letters, B-U-R-N emblazoned on the front and back. During the day it sat on my desk or on the floor and was stored in my safe drawer at night. Once full, I closed the bag and stapled it securely, walked it to the burn shoot where I dispatched it down a

101

steel tube. It traveled into the bowels of the building headed straight for the fiery flames of the incinerator. These tasks eventually became routine, just like Nan and I armoring ourselves for a day's work—girdles, nylons and high heels adorning suits or dresses. At least the days of wearing gloves and hats had passed.

Nan and I fell into easy camaraderie with fellow intelligence workers, with whom we didn't have to keep up a disguise. In retrospect, it seemed rather incestuous, at times unhealthy. In the mid-1960s, the Agency was heavily male-dominated at all levels. Women served primarily in support roles to men in the directorate; this would not begin to change until the 1970s. Powerful and experienced male operations officers often justified questionable behavior on behalf of service to their country. Our social lives revolved around Agency parties and dates.

Christmas parties were particularly dangerous. Each individual country-office planned a party, and all were held on the same day in the headquarters building. No spouses were allowed unless they were already employed by the Agency. Liquor freely flowed, and studly ops officers prowled the halls for easy prey. Careers were made or destroyed in the course of one party. I learned early to keep my wits about me. In the normal course of our days the environment was not as treacherous but it behooved one to be vigilant as I began to prepare for my overseas assignment.

The CIA provided me with credentials and a matching cover story in preparation for my assignment to Cologne. Overseas, our mission was to monitor and gather intelligence on the increasing Russian presence. I lived in a residential apartment in Cologne, rented and furnished by the Agency. I, along with 11 other spooks assigned to work in this new undercover operation, was to blend in.

Our employer bought a beautiful old mansion and turned it into office space for us. A high brick wall surrounded the mansion and its gates were manned by rotating Marine guards.

We hoped the wall served to keep curious Germans guessing about the nature of our work.

Initially, I found work thrilling. On a typical day, I pounded away on my electric typewriter, transcribing reports drafted by my boss. These reports were called dispatches and typically contained secret information about recruited spies or ongoing covert operations conducted in Germany. Occasionally, I participated in stakeouts, and that really got my adrenalin pumping. I quickly learned, however, that surveillance work is often tedious and boring, requiring long, patient hours in all kinds of weather.

On the other hand, invading apartments and bugging them was downright nerve-wracking. My part in these capers was to act as a diversion. Tasked to stroll on the arm of an officer in charge, I chattered quietly about inconsequential things. We cruised past the Russian's apartment a couple of times to ensure the coast was clear, having watched our target as he left his apartment earlier. Satisfied, my partner picked the lock as I shielded him from view. I often contemplated the gravity of this scene, my stomach cartwheeling and droplets of sweat trickling from my armpits. I remember thinking this might be the last thing I ever do. Once inside, we strategically placed listening devices and activated them for optimum results. Within minutes, we calmly exited, leaving no trace.

Social life outside the office was limited to those who worked for the Agency in Bonn or Cologne. I found it lonely and isolating, and missed Nan's company. All the case officers with whom I worked were married men, though most possessed no inhibition about putting the make on the single women in our small contingent. It was as though these men dwelled in a fantasy world: On the one hand, they lived a solid, picturesque, and happy life with a lovely wife and five adorable children; attended Mass every Sunday; and invited their single coworkers, like me, over for holiday dinners. On the other hand, my doorbell ringing at 8 p.m. often signaled an uninvited visit from a married coworker. After this two-year tour of duty, I felt relieved and happy to return to CIA Headquarters in Langley.

When I returned stateside, my new cover story was that I worked as an Army civilian in downtown D.C. in the relatively new Forrestal building. In reality, my assignment returned me to the German desk at Langley headquarters, now as an intelligence assistant. I found my job boring, with little variety. Entire days were spent with my head stuck in dusty case files, work that required almost no interaction with my coworkers. It was like being locked in a closet without a key as the weeks dragged on. Not wanting to go back overseas like most of my colleagues (that was the quickest way to advance professionally) I lived my cover story and settled. In truth, I felt like a translucent jellyfish on the verge of disintegration. The work chaffed at my sense of right and wrong, and I grew progressively weary of living falsely. The very duplicity troubled me. Although, growing up I'd managed to navigate between a secretive family life and maintained a public image, the realization for me was that it no longer fit who I was or wanted to become.

I had found a nice, older apartment on the edge of Georgetown in Washington, D.C., and enjoyed finding odd pieces of furniture to convert it into a home. I'd only been living there two months when a friend and fellow coworker asked if I would consider moving into the house she had just purchased to give her a hand. Nancy's husband was serving in Vietnam, and during a recent skiing holiday she had suffered a spiral fracture to her leg and was in a hard cast from her toes to her hip. She couldn't drive for many weeks, and by moving in, I could be her chauffeur; run errands; and help with cleaning, cooking, laundry, spackling and painting. She offered free rent in exchange.

Just after making this move, Mom finally left Dad in 1968, after many long years of warring. She stayed with Maureen and Dick, who now had two young boys and were living in the little town of Vienna in Northern Virginia. Maureen and her family were scheduled to go overseas by summer's end so this was a temporary arrangement until Mom could find a job and a place of her own. Mom found a nice efficiency in Falls Church and a job at Lord and Taylor department store. She enjoyed her new independence and freedom.

On the other hand—Dad, not so much. He was lonely, cranky, and whiny in my first of many phone calls from him. These calls were unexpected and unwelcomed, much like a toothache. Dad had never been one to pick up the phone for a chat. It was Mom who kept in touch and connected.

"Hello," I said. These were the days before cordless or cell phones, when all calls came to you at home or work.

"Butch, it's Dad."

"Oh my gosh, Dad. How ya doin'?"

"Well, not so good. You know your Mother left me?"

"Yeah, I know. So why do you suppose she did that?" I asked, doubting I'd get a reasonable answer.

"I don't know. But Butch, you've got to get her to come back here."

"Dad, I don't think so. That's between you and Mom. She seems pretty happy. Likes her apartment and her job."

"My God, she has a job! Where? Doing what?" I could hear desperation in his voice.

"Mom's working at Lord and Taylor in sales. She walks to work and lives only a half mile from Aunt Dorothy and Uncle Jonsie. Don't you talk to her?"

"Butch, I can't talk to her. She won't listen to me. I want her to come back," he choked out. "Look Butch, you make a plane reservation, and then get her on the plane. Tie her up if you have to, but get her back to me."

"I'm not doing any such thing, Dad. Let me tell you—it's nice having Mom here—seeing her happy. If you want her back, I think there'll have to be some real changes. And you have to work that out with her."

"Is this any way to treat your Father?" he whined. "I miss her. I'm lonely. Help me, will ya?" Dad asked despairingly, like a drowning man gasping for his last breath. This man, my Dad, who in my 28 years, showed little affection and had no trouble criticizing any one of us with razor sharp sarcasm that left a tearful path of destruction in his wake.

Taking a deep, fortifying breath I said, "Dad, you have to talk to Mom yourself. I'm not getting in the middle of this. I'm not even going to tell her about this conversation. All I know is you've got to make some meaningful changes or she won't listen to you, let alone want to go back to Oregon."

This dialogue went on for months, Dad calling both Maureen and me at least weekly, repeating his demands over and over. It was hard. At this time, there was no Caller ID and each time the phone rang I dreaded answering. Maureen was able to escape with her family for their overseas assignment, but unfortunately that left me to handle Dad's demanding diatribes.

About six months into their separation, I was at Mom's cozy apartment for dinner when she confided, "Pat, I'm thinking about going back to your Dad."

"You can't be serious Mom! Are you?" I was stunned.

"I am."

"But Mom," I sputtered "I thought you liked it here. You've got your apartment looking really nice and your job—isn't that still fun?"

"Well, Pat, it's not as much fun as it was. It's winter now and dark when I come out of work. Maureen and the kids are gone. You're working and have your own friends. I can't be at Dorothy and Jonsie's all the time, and it's not easy making friends here. Besides all that, your Dad really wants me to come home."

Mom had struggled with the winter blues a lot over the years, and this was before vitamin D deficiencies or SAD (seasonal affective disorder) were diagnosed as actual conditions that could leave one's mood as cold and dark as the winter landscape. In the 1960s folks just muddled through or took Valium to help them escape. I could tell that Mom was sliding into a depression.

"Oh, Mom! Do you think things will be different if you go back? I mean do you honestly believe Dad will change his ways?"

"He sounds like he means to. And he has reservations for a Hawaiian cruise he wants to take me on right after the holidays …"

Mom returned to Dad and her life in Hood River. She was reasonably content—for a while.

When Mom returned to Dad, I moved into her apartment. Nancy's leg had healed and her husband was returning home, so the timing was perfect. I lived there for about a year until I learned from a desk mate about a lovely little farmhouse in McLean, Virginia, that he was vacating for an overseas assignment. Nan had just returned from her Berlin assignment, so we decided to move to the farmhouse, which was only about five miles from work.

In the meantime, my CIA-approved social skills advanced. I realized most people were more interested in talking about themselves and learned how to turn any conversation back to whomever I was talking. If that failed, my sarcasm nipped it in the bud.

One fateful evening, found me having drinks at a bar in Georgetown with friends when I met Frank. A tall good-looking man, he sidled up to the bar and ordered a drink. "Hi! What's your name?" he asked.

"Pat. What's yours?" I smiled, cautiously.

"I'm Frank. Mind if I join you?" He wore an expectant, kind smile.

I was unattached, and he was attractive. What could it hurt? "Sure, have a seat."

"Thanks, Pat. Buy you a drink?"

"Sure" I answered.

As we waited for drinks—mine a gimlet, his a scotch on the rocks—Frank chattered, "Where do you work, Pat?"

"For the government." Almost everyone in the Washington, D.C. area works for the U.S. government, but only spooks are evasive about which part of the government.

"Which agency?" Frank persisted.

"Department of the Army, as a civilian. Where do you work?"

"Now that's a coincidence. I work for the Department of the Army too" he enthused. "Where're you assigned?"

"In the Forrestal Building downtown."

"Wow. So do I!" Frank was beside himself.

"Sure you do, Frank. And I'm the President."

"Now wait a minute. I do, and I'm proud of it," he said defensively.

"I bet you are. What do you do that you can talk about? Collect parking tickets?" I laughed derisively.

Looking a little wounded, Frank did his best to answer my question. "I work in budget, Pat. What do you do for the Army?"

"Gosh, Frank, if I told you that I'd probably have to kill you."

"Okay, okay I get it" Frank chuckled. "You must be doing something classified, right?"

"Frank, you're a real Einstein, you know that?" I took another sip of my drink and smiled.

"What floor and room do you work in?"

With a sinking stomach, my brain tried to recall where, indeed, I was supposed to say I worked in the Forrestal Building, hoping against hope he didn't work anywhere near my assigned coat closet. When I provided Frank with the information, his face lit like I'd hung the moon. What were the chances? A nice, good-looking guy, and there I was, armored and on the attack, chewing him up so he didn't get too close.

"That's just two floors down from where I work," he said. We should get together for a coffee next week. What do you say?"

108

"That's a great idea." I wiggled off my barstool. "Hey, it's been great meeting you. Thanks a bunch for the drink. Gotta go."

"But, Pat, your phone number …" Frank looked surprised as he saw me sprint for the door tossing a "bye for now" over my shoulder. I registered Frank's bewildered look, his soft smile, his handsome face, and the droop of his shoulders. I, too, felt like a deflated balloon. I had offered my all-important cover story for the Agency, but wounded a perfectly nice guy in the process. Worst of all, I sensed that Frank possessed a tenderness I would have enjoyed in a future husband, yet at the end of the night—job complete—I was still alone and more discouraged than ever about this duplicitous game.

I avoided sorting out my muddled career by a well-timed visit from Mom and Dad. They had just returned to the United States from visiting Maureen in Vienna, Austria, and decided to celebrate the Christmas holidays with me at my cozy farmhouse. We decorated and threw a lively party, working in harmony on the preparations. Their stay was stress-free and fun until New Year's Eve when Ellen and Tom invited them out for dinner. Reassigned to Headquarters in Langley from an overseas tour of duty, Tom and Ellen were living in Reston, Virginia, a town neighboring the farmhouse. The Mid-Atlantic States rarely saw big snowstorms, but by the time Tom and Ellen arrived that night to pick up Mom and Dad, a foot of the fluffy stuff covered the ground. I had no plans to usher in the New Year, so hung out until I could have the house to myself for the evening. Dad had gotten progressively grumpy through the day, making noises about what a dumb idea it was to go out on such a night.

Ellen waded through the snow to collect our parents, while Tom waited in the car. I greeted her with a warning: "Ellen, Dad's really out of sorts about going out in this weather. You better talk to him. He's upstairs."

She rolled her eyes, knowing she faced a battle. "Thanks for the heads-up," she said over her shoulder as she approached the stairs.

My little farmhouse walls didn't stifle much noise. I listened to the voices raised in anger above me. The situation quickly deteriorated, Ellen on the losing end. Mom wrung her hands, fearing a terrible evening ahead. Dad didn't like Tom, and I figured he was taking out his dislike on Ellen. As I eavesdropped on the bitter words, an image slid into focus in my mind: I imagined myself upstairs with them, facing Dad, as a liberating line in the dirt was drawn.

My shoulders squared as my foot took the first stair. My stomach clenched in dread with my upward progression. I understood what needed to be done if I was ever to be free of Dad's controlling influence. A quick prayer passed my lips that the right words would come. The voices grew louder at my closed bedroom door. A deep breath steadied me, I turned the knob, and swiftly opened the door. My entrance paused their argument.

"You have to stop this yelling," my voice firm and clear. Stunned by the interruption, they gawked at me, Ellen with relief and Dad with annoyance and a flicker of surprise in his hazel eyes. "Dad, Ellen and Tom are trying to make this a nice evening for you and Mom, and you're making everyone feel terrible."

"Now wait just a minute, Butch ..." Dad blustered.

"No. You wait." I let that sink in as I took a calming breath. I looked him unflinchingly in the eye and continued, "This is my house and my rules. If you want to carry on this way, go someplace else to do it. You both need to figure this out in a civil way, and don't come out of this room till you do." I slammed the door behind me, my heart racing so fast it seemed it would surely pop out of my chest. Mom looked up expectantly for some sign— a thumbs up and a hug reassured her. A stiff drink helped calm my quivering nerves.

"Pat, do you think we'll go out in all this snow?" Mom whispered.

"I don't have a clue, Mom. It's up to them now. But if you do, just go to dinner and come right home. You'll be in before it gets really bad out there."

We finally heard the bedroom door open. Mom and I looked at each other anxiously. Ellen and Dad quietly descended to the kitchen, coats in hand and looking rather grim.

"All right, Em. Get your coat. We're going," Dad announced without giving me a glance. As the door closed behind them, my breath whooshed out of me. I took my glass of scotch to the living room and sunk onto the sofa. Simultaneously, I felt euphoric and free after standing up to Dad. This game-changing incident was never mentioned again, but it improved my relationship with my father forever after. It also boosted my confidence, which helped me sort through the path my career should take.

As soon as the holidays were behind me, it was time to set in motion a switch in my career path. Without question, living a lie was disquieting and made me unhappy and a change—not only in my cover story but also in perpetuating both the Higgins family secrets and my own. I liked working for the Agency but needed to do so without all the subterfuge and without working behind a desk, researching for hours on end. Human interaction stimulated my creative juices but my cover story seemed to keep me from the very thing I needed most and was good at. Something had to give.

The Personnel Division (PD) at the Agency was interested in having me, as a former spook; join its team, theorizing that the undercover agents they supported would relate well to me. They did and I thrived in the job of Personnel Specialist, no longer needing to lie. Working in personnel meant being honest and open about working for the Central Intelligence Agency. Sharing with no deception, I finally began forming lifelong friendships inside and outside the office.

Probably for the first time in my 28 years, realization dawned that my coping and communication skills left a path of destruction in my wake. A conscious decision in favor of a healthier life style was in order. First, stop blaming Dad for the glaring faults in my personality and take ownership of all of it, the good and the bad. To this day, I have had fair success banishing sarcasm and putting healthy humor in its place. Still, I slip off the wagon occasionally. It helps that, a few years after my epiphany, a wonderful man came into my life. Before we married we promised to keep sarcasm out of our relationship. After 44 years, we have a successful, loving relationship.

Turn Around Joe

We clustered around a newly constructed, modernistic Dulles International Airport gate in Northern Virginia waiting for our flight to be called. We were a jolly group. Mom, Dad and I were headed to Rome, Italy, for a three-week vacation where Maureen and her husband Dick were stationed. Preparations for the trip had been exhaustive. Any CIA employee stationed like Dick—or like me traveling overseas, went through an intensive briefing before departure to ensure his or her assigned cover would withstand scrutiny. But there were celebratory moments as well that built excitement for the trip.

Ellen and her family of three, Aunt Dorothy, Uncle Jonsie, my cousins Mary and Anne, and Anne's husband Gene gathered to have drinks and dinner and see us off at the gate. This was the longest amount of time I would spend with my parents in many years. I didn't worry about getting along with Mom, but Dad was a different story—our history left a trail of hurt and tears mostly due to his demanding and domineering nature. However, Dad and I had achieved a mutual respect that snowy New Year's Eve two years earlier as we faced-off in O.K. Corral style. Instead of guns blazing and bullets flying, ours was a verbal shootout. Eternally optimistic, I was hopeful that peace would prevail between us all.

Rome's weather was practically balmy compared to the seasonal November weather in America. We shed coats as we schlepped our luggage to the airport curb to hail a taxi. Mom and I hurriedly crawled into the back seat leaving the front for Dad, an action that he never let us forget.

Maureen and Dick's lovely apartment was an hour from the airport, and our driver was a speed demon. Within minutes we realized that all Italian drivers were crazy. On the autostrada he drove 90 mph cutting in and out of traffic, hand hard-pressed to the horn. When we reached the city, the driver jumped the curb and drove down the sidewalk to avoid a traffic tie-up, scattering people everywhere. By this time Mom and I lay prone on the back seat and prayed for deliverance.

Dizzy with relief, we arrived in one piece. We were amazed at the size and grandeur of Maureen's Rome apartment, which afforded each of us our own room. It had four bedrooms and three baths, and it overlooked a central courtyard that contained stunning flora and fauna. Scarlet and fuchsia bougainvillea bloomed profusely against a backdrop of lush emerald greens in the bright November sunshine. In the center of the courtyard was a very large and beautiful swimming pool dotted with Roman statuary. All this boded well for a successful holiday and served to take our minds off the harrowing taxi ride.

Maureen, Dick, Richard, and Stephen had only been living in the city for two months when we arrived. As we settled in, Dad seemed particularly jovial and relaxed. His mood helped us do the same, alleviating the typical Higgins' need to timidly "walk on egg shells" in Dad's presence. Consequently, we frolicked with young Richard and Stephen, both pre-teens, and the household atmosphere was convivial.

Another phenomenon unfolded as the days progressed. Dad couldn't seem to get enough of anything and everything Italian. All my life, Dad had run from and hidden anything to do with his Italian heritage, and we were all instructed to do the same. But now that he was in Italy, literally everything, including the food, was primo, magnifico. I shook my head in wonder relieved he was enjoying himself.

Our Roman holiday was like living a child's fairy tale with no scary parts, except for the flirtatious Italian men. Receiving a pat or pinch on the bum was a common occurrence when navigating the busy Italian streets. Since Dick left for work at the U.S. Embassy each day and the boys were in school, Maureen joined us to explore the famous landmarks of Rome: the Pantheon; the Vatican; the Sistine Chapel filled with the awe-inspiring works of Michelangelo; the Coliseum; the Roman Forum; the Trevi Fountain, which was the setting for the movie *Three*

114

Coins in a Fountain; and the Spanish Steps.

Weary, after several hours of sightseeing, we crossed the Tiber River to the Via Cassia and then to Maureen's apartment in a walled compound of three buildings, which stood, on Piazza Stefano Jacini. Before heading upstairs to the apartment, we stopped at a trattoria, Tavola Calda, which means, "warm table." Trattorias are comparable to our American fast food joints, only vastly different in what they offer. Italians are talented in the way they display food and produce. Each item tempts the tongue and pocketbook. A platter of red peppers displayed on a background of crisp greens looks like a work of art. Prices were very reasonable, so a nutritious feast could be had for a few dollars.

During our second week, Maureen booked us on a three-day trip to see Naples, the Pompeii Ruins, and the world-famous Amalfi Coast. The drive along the Amalfi, built into dramatic seaside cliffs, took our breath away. The roads were extremely narrow and curvy, and they hung above 100-foot drops into the Bay of Naples below. It was slow going, with heavy traffic and crazy Italian drivers, and the road took several hours to traverse. This is not a motorway for the faint of heart. You must possess nerves of steel to attempt it. Our bus driver was an expert at negotiating every obstacle, and we took pleasure in watching him maneuver us through many tight spots. Horns blared, cars backed and juggled for purchase on the cliffs, and hands and arms waved in a language unto itself, effectively conveying friendship and curses.

This excursion included an overnight stay in the picturesque seaside town of Sorrento. Our hotel rooms, across the hall from each other, had balconies suspended, like the roads, precipitously above the sea—but what an awe inspiring and romantic view. After exploring the town and purchasing locally harvested and crafted coral jewelry, we agreed to rest and then meet in the hotel dining room for dinner.

At dinner we enjoyed the delicacies and delicious wine recommended by our young, tall, dark haired, and attentive waiter in the dining room decorated with beautiful works of art. He spoke fair English, and since we were the only ones in the dining room, we engaged in a lively conversation learning little known facts about Sorrento and its customs. Dad particularly enjoyed sparing with him, and in the course of the exchange, mentioned that I was unmarried. Dad thought it humorous when our waiter found reasons to repeatedly brush my shoulder or arms as he served and made suggestive remarks intimating how he could help me pass the long evening ahead.

"Signor Higgins, you stay in this hotel tonight? Yes?"

"That's right. By the way, what's your name?" Dad asked.

"Antonio. And it's been my very great, how you say piacere in English?"

"Pleasure," I said.

"Si, Si, gracia, Signorina. It's a pleasure to serve you. I give you tip to make your stay in this luxury hotel enjoyable. You place your shoes outside your door this evening and I'll see to their, how you say...uuhumm, shine? Okay?"

"Okay." Dad hastened to agree.

"And, Signora and Signorina I bring you at your rooms a special Limoncello. Okay?" Said Antonio.

"Antonio, what's Limoncello?" Mom asked.

"Aaaah Senora, this is very delicious Italian drink. It is our famous liquor made from the rinds of lemons and produced only in Sorrento. Very good for the..." he gestured to his stomach "How you say?"

"Digestion" Mom said helpfully.

"Bueno, good. You will very much like this drink I bring you to your rooms. Okay? Yes?"

"Si, Si," Dad said, trying out the language as I rolled my eyes.

"Antonio, none for me." I interjected. "No Limoncello. Okay?" I hoped this would ward off any amorous attempts. Dad liberally tipped Antonio, and we made our way to our rooms.

116

"Dad, if Antonio tries to make a move on me tonight when he brings that Limoncello, you're going to be in big trouble!" I said with a crooked smile. "You shouldn't have encouraged him like that." At this, Dad's eyes were dancing, and he couldn't suppress a Cheshire grin as he and Mom closed their door. I stood a moment listening to their unbridled laughter, smiling to myself and warmed by this special memory.

I finished my shower and was cuddled up in the luxurious bed when I heard a soft tapping at my door and a whispered, "Signorina, I bring you the special drink." Good for his word, Antonio was at my door. Crossing the room, I softly replied through the door, "Antonio, gracias, but please take the Limoncello away I don't want it."

"Oh, Signorina, open your door. We make nice. Okay?"

"No Antonio, we won't make nice. Go away, now." It took a bit more coaxing before he realized his amorous attempts were in vain.

The next day we enjoyed seeing all the flowers in bloom in November on our return drive to Rome as we headed to Maureen's place to get ready for our Thanksgiving holiday. However, Maureen previously requested that I bring wallpaper and supplies from the States to wallpaper her kitchen, and that had to come first.

I had just completed wallpapering my farmhouse bathroom, so the process was fresh in my mind, and this was my Christmas present to Maureen. As I measured and hung the turquoise flowered paper from my high perch, Mom and Dad assisted with the cutting and paste application, It was a little chaotic, with Maureen trying to prepare minestrone soup for lunch as I straddled the stove, the sink, the refrigerator and whatever else was in my path. The wallpapering took us the better part of a day to complete, but we were pleased with the results. I was especially gratified that a complicated job was accomplished with humor, fun, and no stress.

Turkey Day dawned and Dad, surprising us once again, had a plan. "I'm taking care of the whole Turkey dinner today," he said smugly. It was a family tradition for Dad to prepare the stuffing for the bird, while Mom did the majority of the work: linens, silverware, table decorations, side dishes of green beans, cheesy carrots (her signature dish), Waldorf salad, mashed potatoes, gravy and cheese cake for dessert.

Once the golden-brown turkey, with its succulent aroma, was placed on the table, Dad finished his role by carving it. For me the memory of Dad distributing the crispy, succulent skin triggers a salivary tsunami to this day. But then, back in Oregon, inevitably he shattered the moment like shards of glass as he started a fight with Mom hurling sarcastic words. Maureen's question brought my thoughts back to the present.

"You're really going to do it all?" Maureen questioned skeptically.

"I am, but I have one condition."

"Oh, brother!" we chorused. "What's that?"

"I need you, Maureen, to take everyone, and go to Vatican City. We need some Cannoli's. I haven't eaten any since we've been here and they're my favorite Italian dessert. And while you're at the Vatican pick up some rosaries to take back home for souvenirs."

"You'll do the whole dinner, Dad? Not just the turkey?" Maureen pressed.

"When you get back, let's say—four o'clock—we'll have cocktails and sit down to dinner," he said with a grin. He knew we didn't think he could manage it all.

"Okay, Dad, we're out of here!" I said.

Dad did manage all of it and was in a cheery mood when we returned. In preparing this unforgettable Thanksgiving feast, he gifted us with the most relaxing holiday we could remember. More than that, I glimpsed a warm, generous, funny, loving, and totally unpredictable man during our three-week Roman holiday. I revisit this time often to remind myself that Joe Higgins did possess the qualities I wished for in a father, although they were not often evident.

The Elser family: Mom (Emma Katherine), Grandma,
Grandpa, Aunt Charlotte - Brooklyn, N.Y. ca. 1932 -36

Newly weds, Dad & Mom, 1939

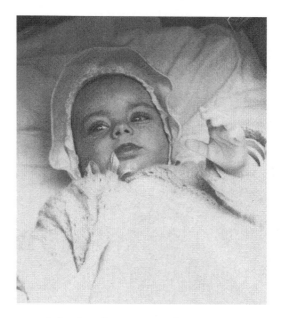

Baby Pat, born December 23, 1941

Ellen, Maureen & Pat
Manhasset, Long Island, New York. 1942-43

Pat & Dad, 1945
Trip across the country to Oregon

Pat at Orchard Road House with Oakie,

Pat, Maureen, Ellen in Easter outfits
made by Mom in 1946

Pat's First Holy Communion - 1948

Shack in Odell before fix-up - Mom in foreground

Odell house after renovation,
interior is completely knotty pine

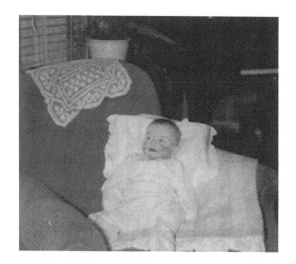

Pete with arm splints and eczema 1949-50

Ellen, Maureen, Pat, Mom and Pete - 1950

Dad & Pete at Columbia Gorge Overlook - 1952

Pete playing cowboy, ca. 1953

Pat's junior year abroad, Vienna, Austria – 1962-63

Wedding Day - May 19, 1974

First home together, McLean, Virginia - 1974

Pat, Bryce, and Brian
Applewood Farm – Summer 1980

Bryce as Halloween Apple - 1983

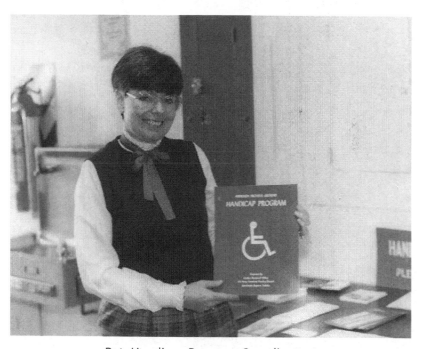

Pat, Handicap Program Coordinator
Aberdeen Proving Ground - ca 1983

Bryce in High School
with Pat and Brian – Ca 1995-96

Bryce, Brian, and Pat - 2005

Family gathering with Mason
Joseph, Oregon – July 2011

Pat on her mule, Celia
Joseph, Oregon – Fall 2010

Wallowa Lake, Joseph, Oregon
Our cabin is at the base of Mt. Howard on the left. Mt
Bonneville, middle and Mt Joseph on the right.

Mysterious Forces

Cars snaked for blocks on that cold February day in 1974. The cause of these long lines was due to an oil embargo imposed a few months before by the Organization of Arab Petroleum Exporting Countries, commonly known as OPEC. This was in response to the American involvement in the Yom Kippur War. Commuters queued at whatever station opened, prepared to wait a long time before reaching a pump. Alternating days to gas up vehicles, as was mandated by the government, fueled tempers and tried patience. Nixon reigned in the White House, Watergate galloped toward full disclosure, and I resided temporarily on Connecticut Avenue for eight weeks and faced this congestion as I traveled from my home in Virginia.

I'd been selected to represent the CIA at a program for high-achieving high school students interested in political science. The program, A Presidential Classroom for Young Americans, still operates today. The students came for a week's immersion in their government's inner workings. They arrived in packs of 200 from every state in the Union and a few foreign countries where they attended schools on military bases. Each week, we started anew with a group of fresh and eager students. Descending on the nation's capital and housed on the second floor of the luxurious and stately Shoreham Hotel, students learned and interacted with the branches of government—not just the three branches of government defined in the American Constitution but also the Press Corps which had distinguished itself by this time in our nation's history as the fourth branch due to its power to influence the American public through television, radio, and print media.

My role had several layers: counselor, tour guide, babysitter, troubleshooter, resource, and model of the life of a "real" federal government employee. Twenty colleagues also represented their agencies, making a composite picture of government at the working level. The bright students examined us to gain knowledge about how government operated in the trenches. It was stimulating and fun to work with teens that came from every socioeconomic, religious, and ideological background imaginable.

That February day we gathered with new instructors to orient them to the Presidential Classroom Program. Most government representatives had no experience working with teens and felt intimidated facing a busload of 25. The students would be divided among 8 buses and the counselors would be responsible for squiring them around for the week. After a long morning, we took a break at Arties, a delightful, cozy Greek pub across from the Shoreham with delicious food.

We sat at a series of small tables connected into one long table. I settled into a green leather bench on one side, and Brian Adelhardt sat opposite of me in a sturdy wooden chair. He was handsome and gregarious, an attractive Lieutenant Junior Grade Officer representing the U.S. Coast Guard. All around, our colleagues chattered. The delectable smells of Arties created an inviting atmosphere on the snowy winter day. I ordered the Rueben, toasted rye bread stacked with tender corned beef, sauerkraut, and a dash of Thousand Island dressing, along with crisp French fries. As we waited for our food, I couldn't help but notice Brian exuded enthusiasm and charm.

"So, Pat where do you live?"

I squirmed. Even though I was the "face" of the CIA for the next few weeks and could be fairly free with personal information, sharing this information wasn't second nature for me. My fingers moved to rub my right earlobe as I contemplated how to answer.

"I live in a little farm house in McLean, Virginia, about five miles from here with my cat, Buffy." My stomach fluttered; my hands began to perspire. So much for small talk. He wanted personal information. I felt like I was about to enter a ring of fire. "How about you, Brian?" I wondered if his interest was real or merely superficial. I thought about similar conversations over the years and expected this, too, might lead to nowhere.

On the surface it appeared Brian had been raised in an idyllic setting, living his whole life in relative ease in and around Baltimore. While not at sea, he lived with his parents as an interim place to hang his hat. His animal menagerie included a couple of horses: Misty was a quarter horse (Brian's first, acquired at age nine), along with Suzy, a frisky thoroughbred. Then there was a dog, Sidney, a personality-plus-golden retriever. His parents lovingly cared for the animals in Brian's absence. Brian openly talked of his two loves: farming and sailing. He dreamed of owning his own farm one day and raising a family. He attended the University of Maryland and graduated with a degree in Animal Science. Once he completed his tour of duty with the Coast Guard, he planned to turn his degree into a farming operation of his own. While Brian didn't have any money, and his parents weren't wealthy, he claimed to have a formula and a prototype to make this happen.

Brian's dreams mirrored my own. I relaxed and enjoyed the open, fun-loving man across from me and found, to my surprise, details about myself began to flow: particulars of my little farm house of five years; my housemate, Buffy, a big calico cat; recruitment into the CIA following my sisters after graduation from Marylhurst College and about living on an apple-and-pear orchard in Oregon from the age of three after being born in New York City.

In the space of a short hour, we discovered we were both single and enjoyed many of the same things, not to mention that we both longed to quit the bureaucratic mumbo jumbo of Washington, D.C. and raise a family in a farm environment.

Lunch ended, and duty and reality reasserted themselves. We headed back across Connecticut Avenue, one of the busiest thoroughfares in D.C. New fallen snow presented a temptation not to be resisted. In the middle of the street, I hastily packed a good-sized snowball and blasted Brian in the back of the head. The war was on...and oh, so much more.

Mid-week of orientation for the instructors, Brian came down with strep throat and went to his parents' home just north of Baltimore to recuperate. His absence created panic among the Presidential Classroom organizers who feared we would be an instructor short for the students first event—a Sunday guided bus tour of Washington, D.C. Every set of adult eyes and ears were needed.

Morning dawned and eight Gold Line Buses queued in front of the Shoreham, two instructors per bus, to herd each busload of 25 charges from place to place on the city tour. We would hit all the highlights: the White House, CIA, Kennedy Center, Treasury, Labor Department, Supreme Court, Capitol Hill, NASA, Justice, Interior, National Arboretum, and more.

My fellow instructor and I were assigned bus number one, and Brian was assigned to bus number four. This group of four buses would travel in tandem during the week, while buses five through eight would travel alternate routes, reducing congestion in an already clogged city.

Ten minutes to departure and there was still no Brian. The staff decided that Brian's partner would have to take the number four bus alone. I stood at the head of the aisle on bus number one, when a fur-collared knight leapt onto the bus. His eyes were all a twinkle. Smiling broadly, he said, "Did you miss me?" Without thought or explanation, I tossed myself into his arms and kissed him soundly on the cheek. He looked as stunned as I, wearing a smile as he departed for his bus.

As the days progressed, a tidal wave of unforeseen, never before experienced feelings and emotions gripped us. Everything stood still as we galloped full tilt. Terrified of the onslaught of jumbled and powerful sensations, unable to sleep, eat, or make coherent sense, I realized I was falling totally and irrevocably in love. It seemed impossible, beyond the pale. Nothing happens that fast, right?

We snatched slivers of time for discovering each other's backgrounds, aspirations and dreams. I learned that Brian had grown up enjoying the water. His parents loved the Chesapeake Bay. When Brian was a teenager, they bought a boat big enough to sleep, cook and cruise the Bay waters and they crabbed, fished and swam all the while. For his high school graduation, Brian's parents gifted him with a 14-foot O'Day Daysailer that spawned his love of the graceful and challenging sport, ultimately leading him into the Coast Guard.

I attempted to unscramble my thoughts and emotions, all the while pulled along into a vortex of sensations—fear, uncertainty, longing and desire. I asked myself, "Am I rationalizing? What am I not seeing? Can he really be the right one for me—complementing those places in me that needed softening?" Delving deep, all the pieces jiggled into place, like a jigsaw puzzle picture of happily ever after.

One evening after the students had retired, Brian and I decided to poke around the grand hotel. From the sweeping lobby to the ballroom to the nooks and crannies, we saw it all. Tiring ourselves out at two in the morning, we ended up in a luxurious ballroom with seating for 1,000 guests. That time of night, it seemed huge and dark, but it was also intimate in the halo of one lone light shining onto the stage. We continued our dialogue about our goals, dreams, likes, and dislikes, taking a break for warm and delicious kisses. Brian wanted to know about my study into graphoanalysis and so, coming up for air, we sat on that stage and embarked on an exploration that changed our lives.

For three years, I'd studied graphoanalysis, the art and science of handwriting and passed basic courses and was nearing completion of my Masters certification. Uncle Jonsie, a master analyst himself, introduced me and suggested the study might help me better understand others and myself. My Presidential Classroom bio, available to all attendees, mentioned this skill and Brian wanted to know more.

"Pat, tell me what you see when looking at someone's handwriting?" He wore an endearing grin.

"Well, I can see things about someone's personality without knowing anything about them."

"How does that work?" Brian asked. Skepticism marked his face.

"When doing an analysis, the writing reveals character and personality traits. I have to be careful to respect the individual's privacy and sensitive to their feelings when discussing what their writing reveals to me. Things may be revealed that only the person who wrote the sample knows about and isn't keen on anyone else knowing." I explained. This was one of my favorite topics.

"Wow," he said. "Tell me more."

"Okay," I smiled. Brian's genuine curiosity reassured me. "No guess work is involved. A complete analysis involves measurement and evaluation of 100 consecutive strokes. That's time-consuming and a tedious process, but it allows me to determine the writer's depth and emotional makeup."

"Wait! You're losing me. What are strokes?"

"Strokes are written lines that are measurable and only the upstrokes are measured. A baseline is drawn and a tool called an Emotional Responsiveness Gauge is used to measure the angle of each upstroke. People have varying degrees of emotional responsiveness. I'm looking at inner reactions rather than actual behavior. Graphoanalysis lets me understand a person's inner emotional makeup. Does that help?"

"Well sort of. Maybe I'd get it if you'd analyze my writing. Would you?"

"I can," I hesitated. "But Brian, it wouldn't be thorough. That takes hours."

"That's okay, I just can't quite believe ..." he paused, letting out a deep breath. "... Well that you're really going to be able to see stuff in my writing. You hardly know me, but I'd like to see how it works."

Reading Brian's handwriting, which I'd never seen, might end our budding relationship before it began. My heart fluttered and began a quick-time beat. I dug out paper and pen. What if I discovered something that ruined it all? What if the writing revealed he was a liar, a cheat, and selfish? Voice prickly with fear, I began. "Okay, I need you to write the following sentence: 'The red fox jumped over the tall brown fence.' And then sign your name the way you would normally."

Brian scribbled the sentence, which, while short, could reveal a good deal. "Okay. Show me what ya got!" He passed me the paper.

Perusing the writing, my pulse raced as I noted the forward slant and heaviness of Brian's writing. "First, I see you've a warmly responsive nature with moderate depth. This means you're generally governed by the way you feel, and if something really affects your emotions, you can go to emotional extremes. However, you do show common sense, pride, and dignity. These traits help keep your emotions in check. Emotional impressions stay with you for a long time, but they eventually fade. This is beneficial because it means you don't hold grudges. You're willing to let hurts go, which is healthy for you."

"Pat, you can see all that?" Brian looked surprised.

"Yes, Brian, and a whole lot more. Do you want me to continue?"

"Absolutely."

"I see that you've a keen and inquisitive mind. You're capable of breaking down information and evaluating a situation when a problem comes up. You prefer a plan of action you're confident you can achieve. This means you often set low goals. They're achievable, but what I see in your writing is that you're capable of much more. Even though you may be outside your comfort zone, you can and do sometimes set distant goals and work with enthusiasm."

Evaluating Brian's writing revealed a basic compatibility in our personalities. The slant and depth of writing are lasting to one's personality and character; only life-altering events might change them. Observing these similar strokes in our handwriting felt comforting and reassured me that we were on a steady course. Brian sat speechless. He later shared that—as comprehension dawned on that cold, March morning—he faced a crossroads. Opposite of him sat a petite, black haired, blue-eyed woman, the opposite of any woman he had previously dated. She could see the very inside of him. She had just told him so, and she wasn't high-tailing it.

The next three weeks were a whirlwind with a new group of 200 students arriving each Saturday afternoon to explore government in action. Action was the key word. Washington could not have provided more drama if it were acting out a Broadway play. Watergate, synonymous with the abuse of power, riveted our nation as it unfolded from 1972 to 1974. Instructors, associated with the Presidential Classroom that year, met and mingled with many key players in that spectacle.

Vice President Gerald Ford addressed the students and staff in a small Senate conference room on Capitol Hill. This man, who would become president in a matter of weeks, offered a warm and sincere, albeit practiced, handshake.

At a private cocktail party in the Shoreham Hotel, I saw Archibald Cox sitting on a stool, nursing his drink. He was the independent Special Prosecutor who precipitated in what became known as the Saturday Night Massacre. President Nixon fired Cox for refusing to do his bidding, resulting in the resignation of the Attorney General and his deputy. Cox seemed larger than life. We were privileged to hear this stately man speak a few words, and we felt honored to occupy the same space with a man who had the courage to stand up to a wrongful order issued by the President of the United States.

One week, Martha Mitchell, wife of President Nixon's campaign manager and former Attorney General, John Mitchell, was guest of honor at the Presidential Classroom formal banquet and dance for students in the Shoreham Hotel Ballroom. Mrs.

Mitchell, colorful and full of self-righteousness, created a stir by making phone calls to the press about matters the Nixon-era conspirators wanted kept under wraps. Mrs. Mitchell strode into the ballroom like an avenging queen decked in pure white sequins and satin, gracing us with her esteemed presence.

Momentum built with each passing day that fateful winter, racing toward a charged finale in every arena: personally, with the mercury of love on the rise as we did our best to carry out our program duties; and important public figures hinted at intrigue as they addressed our students nationally; Watergate unfolded and internationally while the United States tried to extricate itself from Vietnam. All these gathering forces mysteriously pushed and pulled, trying to find purchase.

The intensity of a "moving classroom," both intellectually and socially, drained instructors, and we greatly appreciated a week off to recharge before beginning the final three weeks. Brian and I hoped to spend that week getting to know each other better. However, the Presidential Classroom Executive Director Angie Whittaker, requested that we stay on for that interim week and work the program for the actor Hugh O'Brian. Mr. O'Brian sponsored a program for high school sophomores and wanted the Presidential Classroom experience for his kids. Angie, in her white patent leather boots, black tights, short plaid skirt, and hands-on-hips attitude, said "Pat, you and Brian are our top instructors, and I want the best for Hugh O'Brian! There's a lot of prestige associated with this assignment for you and for the Classroom. Since your agencies have agreed, that's the way it's going to be."

Brian and I respected Angie to a point, but her dictatorial and highhanded manner delivering this backhanded compliment made us wary.

During the Hugh O'Brian week, we had one night off, and Brian asked me to dinner. We dined at the prestigious Polynesian restaurant Trader Vic's in the Hilton Hotel in downtown Washington. A yellow cab whisked us to the restaurant where we sat in a secluded corner. I found it difficult to concentrate on the island décor, let alone the menu. Our hands entwined as we sat close and underneath the table, our feet played footsy. The evening was magical with exotic drinks and island delicacies remembered only through a silky, sensual haze. All was punctuated by sweet and passionate kisses while at the table, inside the elevator, and waiting for the cab. Spontaneous laughter, the sharing, the irresistible pull and magnetic force of those moments served to reinforce how natural and right our relationship felt.

Brian asked the cabbie to "take the long way back" to the Shoreham allowing us to cuddle and kiss in the back seat. The night looked beautiful and misty. Lights reflected and glowed in the dampness. On our arrival Brian said, "Let's walk out on the terrace for awhile."

I was game. I needed to get a grip on the feelings roiling inside me. We walked for a long time through the cold, wet night. The city and hotel shimmered, creating a lovely luminescence. Brian paced us around and around, not speaking. He looked like he had eaten something really bad. I finally spoke up, "Brian, I think we should go in." The mood of the evening had slipped away.

"No, I have something I have to ask you—now just hang on a minute ... I can't breathe ... just give me a minute." Brian took deep breaths, gasping like he was drowning. *For heaven's sake*, I thought. *What's wrong with him? I'm freezing and he looks like he's going to be sick any minute.*

Suddenly Brian burst out, talking fast, "Look I know this is quick, but I think it's the right thing for us...we both agree on so much and have so many of the same goals. So, Pat, will you marry me?"

I was stunned. At 32 years old, I remained the one person in my high school graduating class who had not married. After a scant three weeks knowing Brian, I had not expected a marriage proposal. My relationship track record resembled a minefield. "Mr. Right" never slid into view, until this fairytale like moment. I dared not blink for fear of its loss. The world swirled and glittered around us, a perfect Christmas snow globe, where anything seemed possible.

"Yes, Brian, I'll marry you!" I said, awash with relief and disbelief.

Brian let out a whoosh of air and said, "Okay, great! My God, we're really going to do this?" He picked me up, whirled me around with an exuberant bear hug, and kissed me.

We talked, plotted, and planned until 4 a.m., the outside damp and cold unnoticed. My biggest concern: not having met his family. I thought they might have an issue with the difference in our ages. Brian had told me he was seven years younger than me shortly after we met, and I was concerned about being perceived as "robbing the cradle." Brian optimistically assured me: "Pat, if I love you, I know my parents will love you too. How could they not?"

We didn't want the evening to end. We were on such a high, but we had an early morning ahead of us. Brian walked me to the room I shared with three other female counselors. He tenderly held my face, bending his six-foot one-inch frame down to meet my five-foot-one, and kissed my eager lips in farewell.

Sleep was elusive at best. I pinched myself; my mind whirled and would not be calmed. It all felt so right, but I was scared witless. The next morning, the Hugh O'Brian kids arrived. I will never forget that morning. I had not slept all night. My head spun, stomach churned, excitement built. It was hard to contain myself and remember I had a job to do.

On seeing Brian at the bus queue, under the hotel portico on Wisconsin Avenue, I approached and blurted, "Did what I think happen last night actually happen?"

My head tilted sharply back to plainly see Brian's face. He looked like the cat that got the cream and affirmed, grinning broadly "Yes, you agreed to be my wife."

I returned his smile and sputtered, "But Brian, I'm seven years older than you."

"So?" he asked, totally undaunted.

I worried it would be a huge boulder blocking our path to happiness. I protested, trying to be rational, hand on my hip, "And what about your parents: they've never met me, let alone heard about me. Suddenly, you show up with an older woman who you say you're going to marry?"

Laying his hand gently on my shoulder, Brian soothed and reiterated, "Pat, my mother will love you. How could she not? Our age difference doesn't matter. We've the same goals and religion. We get along great; both my parents'll love you."

At our first stop on the morning tour, the majestic National Cathedral, fellow counselor Fred Bailey, a wise and seasoned representative from the Social Security Administration, wanted to know what was going on. He had observed us gesturing and speaking in hushed tones. We quickly explained, including my concerns. Fred's kind, wide, face broke into a huge smile and he congratulated us both.

"But, Fred, what about the age difference? I'm seven years older than Brian."

"So what? You love one another. Any fool can see that. You both know what you want; you've the same goals and aspirations. I don't see where age makes a difference in this case." Fred sounded absolutely certain.

I felt like a piece of flotsam in a swift current. Brian and I decided to enjoy this extraordinary time, falling deeper in love and planning our upcoming nuptials. We expected our families and friends would be as excited and joyful as we were. The very next weekend, we took the train from Washington's Union Station to Baltimore, where Brian's dad Gilbert, Gil for short, picked us up and drove us to the family home in Baldwin for lunch.

Mr. Adelhardt was warm and welcoming. My nerves eased somewhat as we drove through the gentle rolling countryside in the throes of winter. Trees stood stark and naked, waiting for spring. The Adelhardt red brick rancher, situated a mile north of the tiny two-store town of Baldwin, sat on the cusp of a rolling hill that served as pasture for the horses, Misty and Susie. We entered the home through a jalousie breezeway to find Brian's smiling older sister, Sharon, and his frowning mother, Eileen, arms crossed and looking quite somber.

"Mom, Dad, Sharon," Brian began. "I'd like you to meet Pat Higgins, the woman I intend to marry!"

"But, Brian, what about your future?" Mrs. Adelhardt protested as her hand flew to her breast. My bubble of euphoria drifted away.

Sharon interjected, "Congratulations, brother! I'd a feeling you were going to say something like that when Mother called and told me you were bringing home a girl you wanted them to meet. I wanted to be here to see you for myself, Pat. Welcome to the family."

"Mom, this *is* about my future," Brian said. "Pat and I want to buy a farm and raise our family...that is our future."

"Ahem," Mr. Adelhardt interrupted. "Let's all go downstairs and have a drink to celebrate. Congratulations, son." Mr. Adelhardt shook Brian's hand heartily and broke the tension filling the small breezeway.

We descended to the basement and gathered around a quaint bar decorated in boating and sea memorabilia. Mr. Adelhardt handed me a bracing scotch and water and assured me that this was, indeed, great news. His wife *might* come around, he added, though she had scurried off to the basement laundry room, and I didn't think her absence boded well. Mr. Adelhardt tended bar, secure in his domain, while Brian, Sharon, and I sat on the orange faux leather swivel bar stools. Sharon, tall and portly after the birth of her son Sean, spoke to me in a trying-to-be-hushed voice. Apparently, her mother made her life a living hell before she married Carl.

"She won't be any different this time, you can count on that. Brian's always been the favored child and she won't want to share his attention with you." Mr. Adelhardt and Brian nodded as Sharon continued. "She'll try every trick in the book to get what she wants, just so you know." On hearing this I deflated further, a balloon spent. Brian's optimism had made it all seem so easy.

In spite of this, I was confident love could and would conquer all. Letting myself into the adjacent laundry room, I found Mrs. Adelhardt sequestered in a small, flowered plastic chair watching the laundry rotate through the machine's tiny window. She looked like her world had shifted on its axis.

Sounding braver than I felt, I began. "I'm sorry, Mrs. Adelhardt, that this came as such a shock. I want to assure you that, while it's true that Brian and I have only known each other a few short weeks, we're in love. I intend to do my very best to make him happy." I spoke from my heart the truthful words that had been waiting to unfurl. I wished for a sign of warmth and welcoming. None came.

Whoever said, "love is blind" knew the full force of what this scorned woman would unleash to prevent our wedding from taking place. We picked Sunday, May 19, 1974, as our wedding date, five short weeks away. We decided to marry in Brian's church with a wedding mass and to hold the reception at the Hunt Valley Inn, a short distance from the church. We secured both, and my family would fly in from around the States and Italy.

We gained two very necessary allies in Fathers Bradley and Bayer, the priests who agreed to marry us. I fed Father Bayer a feast of home cooked lasagna, garlic bread, salad, fine red wine and apple pie a` la mode as he counseled us on the makings of a successful marriage. Then, during a solemn interview, we convinced Father Bradley that I was the right woman for Brian. Both priests had known Brian and his family since he was six years old. Laying this groundwork with the priests worked in our favor for when Brian's mom approached both priests and asked that they stop the wedding. They refused.

Her first tactic finding no success, she switched to a frontal attack. Mrs. Adelhardt waylaid me on my arrival at their home one Friday evening. She materialized at my car door before I could get my Chevrolet Camaro stopped. A scowl creased her face as she exclaimed, "You're going to give my husband a heart attack. You know he's got a bad heart and he's very upset about this sudden marriage. You're going to kill him!"

Shaken, I joined Brian and his Dad at the bar downstairs, while his Mom remained in the kitchen preparing dinner. Mr. Adelhardt *did* have high blood pressure, but medication moderated it, and he felt fit as a fiddle.

In contrast, when Brian and I flew to Oregon for a few days after the conclusion of the Presidential Classroom, my mom and dad welcomed Brian with open arms. Brian was barely off the plane when Mom said, "Brian, please call me Kay," giving Brian and I an immediate sense that everything on this front, at least, would be smooth. My parents never questioned the difference in our ages, that we had only known each other two months, or that fate had a hand in our arrangement. All things considered, life seemed pretty unbelievable. Mom and Dad enjoyed Brian, and I felt immensely relieved that he and Dad got along. They talked farming and the stock market as they explored the Hood River Valley together. Brian's ability to make whomever he met feel at ease stood out as one of his gifts.

Mom and I shopped for material for my wedding dress and trousseau. Mom, an excellent seamstress, could put any ensemble together professionally. I wanted a simple, empire style dress: V-neck, tucked in just below the bust with a graceful sweep of fabric to the floor. As Mom worked on the dress one afternoon, her inner fears surfaced.

"Pat, this just doesn't look right. It pooches out too much in front." She wrinkled her brow and peered past me into the full-length mirror in the hallway.

"Mom, it's okay I think it looks fine."

"No it doesn't. People will think you're pregnant!" She tilted her head down, not looking at me.

"Oh, Mom, is that what *you* think?"

"Pat, that *is* what everyone will be thinking or saying … you getting married so fast." I hugged Mom and assured her I was not pregnant.

"Well, the dress makes you look pregnant, so I'm tearing it out and doing it over." And so, she did, three times before she was satisfied that I would not look pregnant for my walk down the aisle. I know she still secretly wondered. And, why not? Her 32-year-old daughter had been dating for a lot of years. Now by some mysterious, unquestionable force, she would finally make a trip to the altar.

Tested

Contrary to the weatherman's promise of bright sunshine, the day dawned gray and drizzly. Our planned outside wedding reception in Cockeysville, Maryland, looked destined to be moved inside. Our path to the altar seemed strewn with obstacles. So far, in the six weeks since Brian proposed, we'd managed to overcome every impediment my soon-to-be mother-in-law threw our way. Yet we both knew challenges lay ahead. Was the dismal weather a precursor of trials soon to be faced?

In retrospect, we both thought an elopement might have resolved everything. Weddings tend to bring out the worst in the immediate family, but they can also produce the best. Like a mule, Brian's mother dug her heels in until Brian gave her *the* ultimatum at four o'clock one morning. He sat at the kitchen bar and ate the breakfast she prepared for him every morning. As he readied to catch his train bound for D.C., his mom nagged relentlessly. "Brian, you need to consider your future. I don't think marrying so fast is right for you. Can't you take time to consider? She's *so* much older than you."

"Mom, look—you're making this impossible! Pat is my future. You have to end these shenanigans. We're getting married and either you accept both of us or you'll *never* see either of us again. If you don't think I mean it—just try me!" Grudgingly, Eileen finally stopped her subversive tactics. While I did not feel she accepted me, I understood that the loss of her son posed more of a threat than she could bear. A tentative truce ensued.

On my side of the family, Dad flatly refused to wear the tuxedo we ordered for him. Two days before the wedding he stonewalled like a spoiled child. "Dad, I'm only getting married once," I said as I stood in the kitchen of my Kirby Road farm house. "Couldn't you manage to do this one thing for me? You look so handsome in that tux."

"Butch, I *don't* like it, I'm *not* comfortable in it, and I'm *not* wearing it." He sulked. My efforts seemed in vain. Mom wrung her hands, envisioning the scene Dad would create.

Brian arrived the next morning and charged forth. He approached Dad in the tiny upstairs guest room. "Joe, what's happening here? About wearing the tux?"

"Those women want to dress me up in that monkey suit, and I don't want to do it, Brian. I feel ridiculous."

"Well, Joe let me give you another take on that. You're giving away your lovely daughter, right?"

"Yes, I am …," Joe said, looking for a trap.

"Don't you think you should at least look on a par with Pat? She'll be beautiful in that dress Kay made. And all the men are wearing formal tuxes. Or do you want to look like an Italian gigolo in street clothes as you hustle your daughter down the aisle?" Brian appealed to Dad's common sense, as well as shaming him a little. "You know you're driving these women crazy with this, but I'm convinced you'll do the right thing—won't you?"

"Wouldn't you like to know?" Dad offered with a sly grin. His eyes twinkled as they shook hands. My theory is that the two alpha adults, Brian's mom and my dad, felt ignored. Brian knew exactly how to handle both situations.

The occasion motivated my family to gather in the same place for the first time in a decade. Dad, Mom, and Pete flew in from Oregon. Ellen and Tom drove from Reston, Virginia, and Maureen, my matron of honor, came from Rome, Italy, where she and Dick were currently stationed. Cousins, aunts, and uncles from New Jersey and New York were also on their way.

Sunday, May 19, 1974, at 4 p.m. in St. John's the Evangelist Church in Long Green Valley, Hydes, Maryland, Joe and Kay Higgins gave me, their youngest daughter Pat, away in marriage at a Catholic mass presided over by Fathers Bradley and Bayer. The small ceremony included only 35 guests. I floated through the arched red doors of the historic church, and the sun broke through the overcast and drizzly sky. I thanked God for erasing the weather obstacle.

Down the aisle we moved, me in the ivory dress triple-sewn by Mom. Its empire lines did not encourage malicious gossip, only praise. It was trimmed in old lace hand stitched by my maternal German grandmother, Lena. I carried a bouquet of fragrant white gardenias and white roses. Dad, dashing in his black tuxedo, and Maureen said he wore a self-satisfied grin all the way down the aisle. The two priests blessed our every move throughout the service, enveloping us in a spiritual armor to protect us in the months and years ahead.

Brian and I breathed a collective sigh of relief as we drove to Hunt Valley Inn for the reception. Drinks and appetizers were enjoyed outside in the flower-decked courtyard. The celebration offered an opportunity for everyone to relax. Guests circulated and visited, catching up on family news. Champagne flowed as we ate fresh Maryland rockfish stuffed with blue crabmeat, and I felt the rightness in my world. I listened and observed as the room hummed with good will, except for Eileen's upside-down smile.

Brian and I said goodbye to everyone, thanking them with a mixture of joy and sadness: joy, because we were ready to realize our dream and raise a family on a farm; sadness for me, because the brief visit with my family left me wondering if we would ever gather again for such a happy occasion. We'd all gotten along and that too was a relief since our family dynamic did not guarantee such a cheerful and pleasant outcome.

Brian and I walked across the hotel lobby to the elevator to go to our room for our wedding night. As the elevator door opened, we realized with astonishment that Father Bayer was accompanying us.

"What're *you* doing?" asked Brian. "Where *are* you going?"

"Well, I've a few more things I want to tell you," replied Father Bayer.

Brian resolutely turned Father Bayer in the opposite direction. "Not tonight you don't," he said. Swish. The doors closed, and we made our escape. To this day we laugh in amazement at Father Bayer's obtuseness. He had said quite enough already to prepare us for what lay ahead. If he'd forgotten something, surely it was too late.

We honeymooned in Vermont, a lovely corner of the country, green and lush like Oregon. We looked for a suitable farm to begin our lives together. Brian loved Vermont and skied there often through high school and college. The topography was reminiscent of Oregon, but I thought the winters too long and harsh, and the ground was strewn with rocks. Looking for real estate became a recurring theme in the years ahead. We both relished the possibilities presented by an old house, a secluded woodsy cabin, or a sprawling piece of land on the Chesapeake Bay. I learned quickly that Brian, undaunted by risk, thrilled to a challenge. I, too, savored the stimulation and adventure of our new goals, but needed Brian's enthusiasm and daring-do to help me take that leap.

After our honeymoon, we settled into the small four-room farmhouse I rented in McLean, Virginia. Five years earlier when my CIA office mate transferred overseas, his landlady, Jessie MacIntosh, a widow retired from government work, wanted a new tenant. "Mrs. Mac" and her late husband acquired a lot of property in the affluent area, where diplomats and politicians made homes on quiet estates. The farmhouse was ideally located, just $75 a month for a house, barn, and five acres. A treasure. I quickly jumped at the chance to rent it, and Mrs. Mac and I formed a bond that endured the rest of her life. When Brian entered the picture, he and Mrs. Mac instantly hit it off.

"Glad to meet you, Brian. Pat tells me you're a serviceman." Mrs. Mac said.

"That's right, U.S. Coast Guard. It's a pleasure to meet you too and Pat's told me a lot about the nice things you've done for her over the years."

"Well, I don't know about that. I've enjoyed having her next door and we look out for each other."

"Mrs. Mac, since I'm moving in we're going to give you a raise in the rent to $100.00. Pat told me that when her roommate, Nan, moved out you lowered her rent so we think it only fair." Brian explained.

"Well my word, goodness sakes. You surely don't have to do that." Mrs. Mac protested with a look of amazement. Mrs. Mac often called Brian "my Maryland boy" and they got along famously.

We loved it there, but we knew we needed more. Most weekends were devoted to our hunt for a farm that we could call our own. Brian really wanted to find land in Maryland after realizing Vermont was not practical, and I agreed. I liked the rolling hills and moderate climate that exuded a quiet, gentle beauty, such a contrast to the dramatic landscapes of Northwest Oregon. Within nine months we secured a Farmers Home Administration loan. Our real estate agent, Phil Carlton, found one hundred acres of rich farmland.

"Brian and Pat, this piece of property straddles the Mason Dixon Line, which forms the Maryland-Pennsylvania border." Phil said.

"What determines which state you use for an address?" I asked.

"It's where you lay your head at night. With this property there's no question since the old farmhouse and all the outbuildings are in Maryland." Carl explained. "Besides the house, outbuildings include an old barn, two corncribs, a well house, and chicken coop—all in need of repair. The farmhouse was built in the 1700s and positioned just below the lip of a rolling hill, facing south."

Evergreens were planted behind the house to afford protection from the north winds. Deciduous trees strategically shaded the front from the searing summer heat but allowed in the natural warmth of the winter sun as they shed their leaves. I thought it brilliant that farmers in the 1700s knew to take such advantage of the lay of the land. By 1975, society seemed to ignore the benefits of natural surroundings. A sense of wellbeing enveloped me. Even though we planned a big jump, these little reassurances helped me prepare for the challenge ahead.

One morning, we met Phil over coffee at the local Whiteford diner, the town where the farm was located. Our intention was to check on how things looked and finalize buying the farm. Phil began, "You know when looking at farm acreage you look for land with good attributes for growing crops, right?"

"Well, of course, that makes sense Phil, so what's your point?" I asked.

"The point is, Pat, if the property includes a house and outbuildings so much the better, *but* the condition of these structures is incidental," Phil explained.

"Do you mean if the house is in a shambles it doesn't matter, because the land is a good deal?" Phil nodded in the affirmative.

"I'm not living off the land, you know!" I felt my blood pressure rising. "I want to see the inside of that house before we go to settlement. You guys both understand that, right?"

"Okay, Butch, if that'll make you feel better, I'm sure Phil can make that happen. Right Phil?" Brian said.

Within a week, Phil arranged for us to see the inside but cautioned, "This has to be short and sweet because the current tenant is still in the place and isn't happy about giving access. Also, he's not the most pleasant guy either."

Before the walkthrough, we learned from local scuttlebutt that previous renters included folks who raised racehorses; farmers arrested for growing marijuana; dog breeders who used the upstairs rooms for kennels; and the current occupant, who made a practice of shooting every bird in sight. Brian and I both felt uneasy about what we might find.

Eerie silence reigned that day. We drove slowly down the farm's half-mile lane off of Prospect Road, taking in the rolling landscape with hope. As we approached the house, a scene greeted us that took my breath away. I gasped, "Oh, my, Brian what do we do now?" Straight out of a western movie, the renter blocked the drive, his stance wide and belligerent. A rifle hung at his side.

"Oh, shit! Just take it easy, Butch, we've a contract on the place and told we've access. It'll be fine." Brian sounded like he was trying to convince us both. We exited the car, smiles plastered.

"Hello Mr. Taylor. I hope you got the word we're to get a look inside the house today" Brian said.

"Yeah, I heard." The tenant spat a brown putrid tobacco wad at our feet. I felt faint with anxiety, but Brian seemed undaunted. "You can go in, but make it quick 'cause I got someplace I gotta be."

"We'll do that, thanks," said Brian.

On the blitz tour, we found the house had four upstairs bedrooms painted fuchsia, pee yellow, peacock blue, and lavender—each pockmarked with holes and scratch marks from canine residents. The single bathroom, carved out of a larger room, was graced with an electrical fuse box resting directly over the claw-foot bathtub. The peeling and water-stained wallpaper in the upstairs hallway could only be described as toxic tan. The kitchen, long and narrow, held a porcelain sink with chipped washboard drains on each side, one tiny cupboard, and undulating floorboards. We didn't venture beyond the basement door; that daunting black hole could wait for future exploration.

As we drove quickly away, tears streamed down my face. Brian, the eternal optimist, tried to reassure me, "It has a lot of potential," he said. "You'll see."

"Brian, we're going to have to live in that place. It's a mess! Do you think we're really doing the right thing?"

"Trust me. We're getting a really good deal on that piece of land. I'm sure our FHA loan officer will loan us money to fix up the house if we need it. In the meantime, imagine what some soap, water, elbow grease, and paint will do," Brian said.

Settlement on 4435 Prospect Road, Whiteford, Maryland, took place on March 31, 1975, and my conviction that I loved a challenge began its true test.

At this time, the nation faced nearly a decade of low economic growth, and separating from our secure government jobs felt like jumping without a parachute.

"Brian, do you really think I should quit my job? I'm not having any luck lining something up within commuting distance of the farm."

"Yes I do. I know it's scary to do it without either of us having a job. But something will turn up." We had our FHA loan to purchase the real estate, but our meager savings were eaten up with the purchase of machinery, which was needed as soon as we moved in April—planting season. We proceeded with faith and conviction. Together, we could do anything.

Torrential rain and shrieking wind blew out store windows and downed trees the day we moved in. I often wondered if the weather forecasted a future of strife, uncertainty, and hardship. It was, after all, April Fool's Day, 1975.

When Brian graduated from the University of Maryland with a degree in animal science in 1971, he planned to raise Black Angus cattle when he found his farm. However, first we needed a tractor, corn planter, mower, truck, and, of course, the cattle. Up to this point, we'd managed to procure everything except for the cattle.

Brian led our small caravan from Kirby Road in the big red international farm truck loaded with our possessions, including gallons of eggshell-white paint to coat the colorful upstairs walls. Uncle Jonsie, a Duron paint salesman in Arlington, Virginia, had gifted us with a cache. Because Brian was entitled to one shipment of household goods at the end of his Coast Guard service, the bulk of our belongings would arrive in a week. This allowed time to sweep, clean, and paint the farmhouse while we slept at Brian's folks' house.

Buffy, the cat, and I followed the truck in my low-slung orange Camaro, completely inappropriate for traversing fallen branches and the rough, potholed farm lane—but it had to do. Wind and rain lashed and rocked the car. I talked reassuringly to Buffy in the carrying cage beside me. "Buffy, it's going to be all right, you'll see. We'll make this a great adventure. I saw lots of mice and rats for you to hunt in that great big barn as you get to know the place." I grimaced, as I continued. "I'm sure there are plenty in the house too."

Those first spring weeks on the farm, I felt like Dorothy in the Wizard of Oz when she realizes she isn't in Kansas anymore. Many new discoveries bewildered us like black snakes dropping unexpectedly out of the willow tree next to the house or slithering in the basement. Gil, Brian's father, was the only one brave enough to explore that "black hole," assessing the state of the oil furnace. I can still see him emerging from his first foray, climbing up the ladder like a Halloween scare. He was covered in cobwebs, sporting a huge smile and shaking his head at the unbelievable task we had undertaken. "Well that was something. That basement is all damp dirt. I found the old furnace which I think will work and I'm calling it Igor." He said with a good-natured laugh.

Eileen and Gil lived only a half hour's drive away and she offered to go with me to help clean up the old farmhouse. I attempted to forge our truce as we dusted, mopped, scraped, spackled, and painted. She often brought nutritious picnics that we consumed ravenously during quick lunch breaks. We all shared the common goal of turning the dilapidated dwelling and outbuildings into something livable. One week later, our goods arrived and move in we did—just as Brian flew off to a U.S. Pony Club board meeting in Chicago. I was on my own with all the critters yet to be revealed.

We sat at a small table under the west living room window of the farmhouse, just finishing the lunch she had prepared when Eileen suggested, "Pat, you come and stay with us while Brian's gone. He says you're planning on staying here all by yourself." Eileen had never stayed anywhere by herself at anytime in her life and couldn't imagine my doing so.

"Thanks, but no thanks" I replied. "I think I'll be just fine now that we've electricity and water. While Brian's gone, I plan to clean the wainscoting on the living room ceiling with 409 and get that black soot off. It'll probably take me exactly as long as he's away. It's a pretty big room."

I was not happy Brian had left his ten-months-new bride alone with who knew what. However, I did not intend on sharing that with Eileen who, I knew, still hoped to work my discomfort to her advantage. But my goodness, the indigo night, so dark. The evening noises were like a symphony, magnified and exotic. Our farmhouse was a half-mile off the road, and the closest neighbor just as far. No ambient light from the town of Whiteford, five miles away, or Bel Air, 14 miles distant, brightened the sky. Barely-can-see-your-nose-in-front-of-your-face dark. The stars and moon sparkled brilliantly against their black backdrop, offering some illuminated relief.

I listened for approaching danger, but none came. Hard work, and plenty of it, kept the boogeyman at bay, and I survived, much to Eileen's chagrin. I wonder if I had more guts than sense.

One night after Brian's return, we experienced our first financial epiphany. We sat on our king-sized bed looking mournfully at each other. What had we done, leaving our secure government jobs with benefits? We banked my whole salary during the ten months we searched for the right farm, but now we were almost down to our last dollar. Before we left our jobs, I'd applied for a position at a U.S. Army installation, Aberdeen Proving Ground that was 20 miles southeast of the farm. However, no positions were available. The CIA granted me six months of paid leave with benefits. Then I could go on leave without pay for up to a year, so I would not have a break in federal service—which meant I could keep accruing retirement, benefits, and pay without starting from scratch again—if I could find a job before that year was up.

We were only three weeks into home ownership, and we had spent our cushion, which had proved to not be nearly enough. There would be no Black Angus cattle bought that year. Brian needed to find a job off the farm, even though we were both swamped with work on the farm. Fields needed tilling and planting; it was April after all. Nothing to do but revert back to our unshakeable belief that "together we could do anything." We just need not panic. Brian gratefully accepted a minimum wage job at Tidewater Marina putting dock pilings in the Chesapeake Bay. Unafraid of hard, dirty work, Brian came home each night only to jump on the red International Harvester tractor and disc our beloved fields until dark.

Just six weeks after we created this economic tsunami in our lives, our first anniversary loomed on the horizon: May 19, 1975. No extra cash existed. I figured it would be a non-event. Oh, contraire! My prince announced that morning that I was to be dressed to the "nines" when he got off the tractor that evening. We sat eating a quick breakfast before Brian headed out to the marina. "Butch, we're going to dinner and celebrate our first anniversary."

"Brian, you know we don't have the money for a night on the town."

"Look, this is our first anniversary. We're going to put it on the credit card and figure it out later. I'm not taking no for an answer," declared Brian. I surprised myself when I realized that while I was deeply worried about our financial situation, I warmed at Brian's chivalry and romance.

We started the celebration at Pierce's Plantation sipping mint juleps. Brian had introduced me to this luscious concoction before our wedding, and Pierce's was a favorite Adelhardt watering hole. The julep glasses were glazed to the top with frosty layers of ice; filled with smooth, mellow bourbon; and crowned with fresh, fragrant mint. Our next stop was The Hunt Valley Inn, the scene of our wedding reception the previous year. We enjoyed a delectable and romantic dinner with much too much wine, accounting for the fact that I can't remember what we ate. To this day that special evening evokes wondrous, starry-eyed warmth. Left on my own, I would have squelched this respite from our labors of turning the farm into our home.

We were settling in and getting a feel for our farm by taking long evening walks. We were anxious to follow local custom and find an appropriate name for the farm. There were six ancient apple trees to the left of the house that recalled my childhood on an apple-and-pear-orchard. After a lot of deliberation, we liked the sound and feel of the name "Applewood Farm."

Working to make Applewood Farm livable, we hauled 38 truckloads of trash to the dump that spring. Inside the house we cleaned and painted. Outside we plowed, disked, planted, and fertilized the corn crop. Our animal population included a golden retriever named Sidney, 16-pound Buffy, the mentally challenged thoroughbred Suzy; quarter horse matriarch Misty; red foxes with curious cubs; a stately pheasant; musical spring peepers; whitetail deer; and an unhealthy number of snakes, rats, and groundhogs in all stages of procreation.

No task seemed beyond our reach in those early days. I read in the local paper that the Forest Service was offering free tree seedlings to anyone who had a quarter of an acre or more to plant them for reforestation.

"Brian, look at this" I said. "It says if we plant these seedlings we can sell them for Christmas trees when they reach maturity in seven to eight years. What do you think?"

"Sounds like a thought," he said. "We have that area along the creek that isn't tillable. Why don't you call and see what the story is?"

I knew nothing about evergreens. I convinced myself that the unknown was part of our adventure and dialed.

"Mrs. Adelhardt, I'm glad you called. We've thousands of seedlings available for the taking. How much ground do you have?" asked the Forestry Project Officer, Wayne Merkel.

"We figure about a half-acre down in our meadow along our creek. Can we sell them as Christmas trees as they mature?" I asked. I hoped we could start a nest egg for the family we soon hoped to start. "Mr. Merkel, we know nothing about raising Christmas trees but we're willing to learn."

"No problem. You'll catch on. We recommend you plant the seedlings on 7-to 8- foot centers, but they still tend to crowd one another as they grow so you're permitted to sell those that you thin out."

"That sounds good," I said.

"You know any ground you put into Christmas trees can qualify you for substantial tax benefits?" Wayne encouraged. "You can plant one thousand seedlings on that ground you picked and we have the tree spades to loan you as well."

How hard could that be? Little did I know it would cause strife in this perfect union. We hadn't accounted for rocky, weedy soil and the backbreaking work required to jump on a tree spade and wiggle a hole big enough to receive a seedling. One thousand times.

Brian's frustration over this process revealed vulnerability in me. As I listened, I feared that any disagreement might tear our relationship irreparably. We were only a year into our marriage, and as irrational as it was, I was scared that Brian might find me wanting because I found myself wanting. How could he be that much in love with me, an older woman by seven years? I quickly tamped down these feelings of inadequacy, masking them from Brian, thinking it my responsibility to keep our union intact.

Despite the hard work and concerns, we both found it very satisfying to watch our newly planted trees take hold and grow. Like the trees, our relationship grew and deepened, and so did my sense of trust. I gained confidence little by little as I unveiled bits of my hidden past.

These Little Piggies Go to Market

By our third year on the farm, we managed to clear out the trash and debris from the lower barn. There was much less to deal with than what we faced initially, so only two truck loads went to the dump. Brian decided the back corner was an ideal spot to raise some feeder pigs for the freezer trade.

The barn had a cement floor throughout, which was the perfect flooring to keep a pen clean and sanitary for the piggies. Brian used fence panels to construct the pen. He added feed and water troughs and rigged a water supply to hose the pen daily, clearing it of waste. Next, Brian brought home ten pink and adorable 20-pound piglets. We leaned on the fence panels and watched them scurry about exploring their new home, oinking, snuffling and no doubt trying to find their mom.

"Butch, we can't name these little guys," Brian cautioned.

"Well, darn, they're sure cute and I bet they're missing their mom."

"They might be but I kind'a doubt it."

"Why's that? I asked.

"Butch, they've been farrowed and weaned, which means they've been separated from their mom for a few weeks. Once that happens, they're called feeder pigs and are sold to finishers. That's us. We'll finish them out, and in about four months, they'll be perfect and ready for our new business."

"Does that mean they're off to the slaughterhouse?" I hesitantly asked, looking at these darling little creatures and feeling like the grim reaper.

"Yup, that's exactly what it means and it's a good reason not to get attached. Okay?"

I nodded solemnly, attempting to harden my heart.

As an Animal Science major in college, Brian knew what needed to be done when it came to raising pigs. He also had hands-on experience helping his college friend, Ronnie Garner, establish his pig farrowing operation on Maryland's eastern shore. I knew nothing. My animal experience was limited to dogs, cats and an occasional parakeet or canary. The freezer trade was also a new concept to me. The way Brian explained it, when the pigs reached a weight of about 200 pounds, they'd be ready for market. He would raise the animals, feeding them ground ear corn and protein supplements. I would be in charge of marketing and selling the meat, which we'd offer by individual cuts. I anticipated a ready market at Aberdeen Proving Ground where I had finally managed to find a job after 4 years. I floated the concept past my three carpool buddies who showed real enthusiasm for the idea. They liked not having to go to the store for their meat. It was premature in 1978 for any of us to be concerned about where and how our food was produced, but the shopping convenience and corn-fed pork was the attraction and made everyone's mouth water in anticipation.

In August the no-name pigs were ready. As luck would have it, Brian was in the middle of the corn harvest at Whiteford Packing Company, a frozen food pant where he had gotten a job, and he couldn't get away. Gil and I were put in charge of the pig harvest, and I'm not sure who knew less. I called Maureen, who was now living two hours away in Vienna, Virginia, to come with her teenage sons, Richard and Stephen, to help.

The day dawned hot and humid, and the weather forecaster promised that the temperature would soar to the 90s. Brian rose early to make sure everything was ready in the barn for the harvest. Because of the predicted heat, he amply watered the pigs. Maureen and the boys arrived the previous night, and once breakfast was over and Gil arrived, we were ready to begin.

Brian had built a chute with high sides that hooked on to the back of the 1500 one-ton International truck, which Gil backed to the entrance of the barn. We developed a strategy for opening the gate to begin ushering the 200-pound pigs to the chute. Equipped with strong sticks and rubber boots, we positioned ourselves in gauntlet formation outside the pigpen door.

164

At this point the pigs sensed our nervousness. Pigs are smart and I was giving off alarm vibrations. They were on their feet and shuffling around their pen. The weight of the responsibility for successfully bringing these pigs to market terrified me. I was ill equipped for the job. In fact, not one of the five of us knew what to expect. We hoped the pigs would calmly walk to the chute and up into the truck for their trip to the slaughterhouse.

A pig squeals at 115 decibels. A jet engine's sound is around 113 decibels. Pigs can run like the wind and do a mile in seven minutes. All this became clear as the pig gate opened. There was no orderly progression. Pig screams deafened the air, drowning out my own screams as I tried to give the crew some direction. The 10 pigs ran everywhere except in the direction of the chute, and we stayed in hot pursuit, slipping and sliding in pig shit. After what seemed like an eternity, we stopped running and prodding to catch our breath. We looked at each other and realized the pigs had outsmarted us. Did they know where they were headed? I started laughing, somewhat hysterically. Maureen, Steve, Richard, and Gil joined in, and once we started, we couldn't stop. The laughter relieved the tension. We vowed to take a calmer approach in our second attempt.

This proved no more successful, and the squeals filling the air will live in our memories forever. At one point we did succeed in getting two of the pigs up the ramp, only to have the second one take an about face and vault himself over the high side, right into Gil, almost knocking him over. What a sight. By now, the pigs, and we were hot, tired, dirty, and sweaty. An unspoken truce ensued, and our third attempt succeeded in getting every pig loaded onto the truck and the back gate secured.

Gil pulled the truck into a shady spot to keep the pigs comfortable. We took a lunch break to calm ourselves and cool down. Afterwards, Maureen and the boys needed to head back to Virginia. After Gil had hoisted himself up to peer into the truck bed I heard his excited "Whoop! Whoop! Whoop!"

"What's wrong?" I asked, knowing that this was not going to be good.

"One of the pigs is dead, Pat."

"Oh no," I moaned.

"We'd best get rolling before we lose anymore," Gil said as he jumped down and headed for the driver's side. He revved up the truck, and we headed out the lane for the 20-mile drive to the slaughterhouse. We were both quiet, reflecting on this latest trauma of the day. Tears started streaming down my face as I looked at Gil.

"I don't want to be the boss of this! I don't know what I'm doing," I sobbed.

"Now, now, Pat. You did the best you could. We both did. Something went really wrong with this whole fiasco, but it wasn't your fault."

Continuing to sob, I choked out, "But the pig died. Do you think they know where we are taking them? That squeal—so human and they're smart."

Gil patted my shoulder sympathetically, trying to calm me, but I was inconsolable.

"I don't want to be in charge. Brian should've been here," I wailed.

As we reached our destination, I managed to stop the teary torrent and conduct our business with the butcher. Gil and I sighed with relief as the rest of our cargo calmly exited the truck for its final, grisly destination.

Frayed Edges

Our early days on the farm were filled with highs and lows. I never thought of myself as one prone to depression, but farm life taught me new things about myself. The grinding weight of financial insecurity wore me down. In all my 33 years, I never missed paying a bill on time or needed to pinch my pennies. Life on the farm changed that.

One day, I stood at the pantry door of the farmhouse kitchen, more than a little worried about what to cook for dinner. I took stock: peanut butter, one can of tuna fish, cream of mushroom soup, pasta. A pitiful inventory for a pantry with six shelves. The reality of a bare cupboard and an empty freezer hit me like a rogue wave heading for shore. Everything tumbled in its path. Insecurity and terror descended as I recognized the clear reality of our meager circumstances. Everything we earned went toward paying the mountain of bills we had accumulated. Food, it seemed ranked low on the priority list.

Moments later the propane deliveryman arrived to fill our tanks. He knocked loudly at the door and shouted "Mrs. Adelhardt, are ya home?"

Puzzled by the interruption, I opened the back door to find a 30-something year old man. Behind him a truck was parked with a familiar gas company logo. "What can I do for you?" I said, a little wary.

"You have an outstanding bill with Delta Gas, didja know that? Over $100. Can't fill y'r tanks if you don't pay it."

Flabbergasted I sputtered, "We've never received anything that indicated we're behind in our payments. I don't understand."

"Well, it's a fact. But I could help you out with this if you'd let me."

"What do you mean?"

"If you let me in so we can talk about it, I'll explain what I've in mind."

"I don't have time right now. I'll call Mr. Jones and discuss our bill with him. I didn't know we had an outstanding balance, but we'll make sure it's taken care of immediately." I blushed with embarrassment and closed the door. It was mortifying to realize we gained a reputation of delinquency and I was unnerved by the service man with his own agenda. While we anticipated a monthly bill from the gas company, they expected us to pay from the receipt stuck in the door upon delivery. We hadn't always found a receipt, thanks to the wind and haphazard delivery schedules. After I called and explained what happened, Mr. Jones allowed us to pay the balance a little at a time and reprimanded Bill, the deliveryman, for trying to deliver more than propane. Apparently, I wasn't the only woman-of-the-house Bill offered to "help out."

Brian and I had been raised with different philosophies when it came to money. Dad and Mom taught me to be responsible and careful with my money. It was understood that once college graduation rolled around, I would be on my own. The thought of approaching them for a loan never crossed my mind. Brian had no such qualms about asking his parents for help when things got dire. Asking for a handout rattled me to my core. True, Brian never asked unless we had nowhere else to turn, and his parents were gracious and generous. However, being in an asking position chipped away at my equilibrium. We had no resources with which to work on repairs on our old farmhouse and this was an area where Brian felt he should ask his parents help.

We knew that the first thing that needed fixing was the foundation. This major summer project of putting in a basement began with our old log house being lifted by house movers. The movers literally lifted it up and off its foundation, then braced it in place with steel beams. Next, our neighbor George Miller, a master fixer of all things mechanical, brought his bulldozer and drove down the dirt ramp, in and out under the house. George skillfully cleared out all the caved in dirt and scraped back the sides. Next step was to haul, mix, heft, and lay concrete blocks—all while we continued to live in the house. We used narrow board planks over the abyss to gain access. The house movers gave us six weeks to get the job done before they would be back to set the house down and pull the steel beams. We called everyone we knew to give us a hand. Brian, I and sometimes Gil, worked at nights. On weekends our legion of friends pitched in. Every one of us worked full time jobs, and we all brought a sense of urgency to finish the project on time.

Concurrently, the fieldwork needed attention, and that year Brian decided we would till the corn rather than use herbicides. On the weekends, I cooked for our crew of friends and family and, between meals, tilled rows of corn with our tractor. The International 756 tractor was large. Getting to the seat, maneuvering the gears, and steering the tiller around challenged me. Three weeks into the routine, two startling events happened.

After cleaning up lunch dishes one day and making sure dinner bubbled in the crockpot, I headed back out to the cornfield. I chugged along on the tractor and saw that turning under the oak tree—with its low branches—looked like a tight squeeze. Backing and pulling forward a couple times, lining the tractor and tiller up in the next four rows, I hit the throttle, eased the clutch, and off I went. A large wasp nest hung in the direct path of the tractor's smoke stack. I swerved, but too late.

"Oh shit!" I hollered, jamming on the brakes. "Oh shit! Ooowwwhaa!" I screamed. A wasp dove for the tender flesh of my exposed arm and found his mark. I shut down the tractor and scrambled down the tiny steps, knowing the whole hive would soon join the attack.

When I turned 28 years old, I'd developed a severe allergic reaction to bee stings. Because I'd experienced a bout with anaphylactic shock, my body swelling beyond recognition, my doctor advised when stung: "Try to stay calm, take Benadryl, put toothpaste directly on the sting, then icepacks. Next, give yourself a shot of adrenalin—I carried an Epi pen for that purpose—and lie still. If you start swelling call an ambulance."

This day, with the wasp's nest, I was on the back forty acres of the farm, at least a quarter mile to the house. Staying calm seemed out of the question. I eluded the rest of the hive, but their agitated buzzing motivated me to sprint for safety. Once in the house, I plunged the syringe of Epinephrine into my thigh—waited and wondered if we were crazy trying to turn Applewood Farm into a going concern. Thankfully, the shot did its job and kept the swelling localized.

The second noteworthy event occurred that same day. For our basement, our team of family and friends mixed cement, measured, and laid concrete blocks, now up to the fourth row and right on schedule. What the workers didn't realize was that they were displacing former residents. Those residents picked that afternoon to reclaim their home by slithering quietly over the new blocks filling the space. Brian told me later, as one of the workers reached to pick up his next block, he let out an uncharacteristic shout. He then jumped trying to avoid an eight-foot black snake comfortably coiled in the waiting blocks. Everyone working in the basement joined together, exorcising the snake and his companions with pitchforks. It was a reptile roundup for the record books.

During those six long weeks, as the rows of blocks grew, we experienced a rare earthquake that shook the ground and swayed the house. We prayed for calm, quiet, dry weather but still endured several summer thunderstorms, causing our saturated, loamy soil to crumble. Supports shifted. One evening while at the stove cooking, the floor under the stove suddenly dipped dangerously downward. I called George next door:

"George, I think we've an emergency here! The kitchen seems to be caving into the basement. Can you come take a look?"

George's typical speed is a notch below slow. He came within the hour. By that time, Brian was already in the basement assessing the situation.

"Well you've a problem here," drawled George. "Good thing I left the dozer here. Let me run 'er through, and we'll let the bucket support the kitchen while we build a column of blocks to hold a jack to keep 'er in place for now," Brian and I looked at each other. What else would go wrong? George revved up the oil belching dozer and very carefully drove it in under the house, threading the eye of a needle. Black smoke puffed into the rooms above. Again, George salvaged a difficult situation so that we could continue to complete the basement walls in the time allotted. Right on schedule the house movers came and sat our house down on its new foundation.

There was still a lot to do in the basement. After dinner one evening, Brian and I were preparing for the concrete floor to be poured the next day. We tried our best to jockey around a 50-pound, 20-foot-long wood beam. It was awkward and way more than I could safely handle. The beam's intended destination was a hole in the chimney, previously occupied by a steel beam that the house movers removed. Brian rigged one end of the beam in the hole. Wire held it tenuously as we maneuvered a lolly-column into place for support. Brian climbed the ladder. He steadied himself by placing his hand in the hole intended for the wood beam. Below, I struggled to stabilize the other end of the beam. A friend, Don helped.

"Goddamn it! Motherfucker," hollered Brian as the board jolted in our hands. Don and I looked at Brian in alarm, his face twisted in pain. He gripped his right hand, teeth clenched, grimacing. He whispered, "Fucking wire broke—smashed my middle finger."

We packed Brian's hand in ice, but the set of his jaw and the look in his eyes confirmed he was suffering. Sprinting to the car, Don convinced me that he should drive. A mistake. The race to the hospital, 30 minutes from the farm along country roads, proved harrowing. He drove like a turtle crossing the road. The trip seemed like 30 hours. As luck would have it, the orthopedic surgeon on duty that night at Harford Memorial Hospital was Dr.

Green. He thrilled to the challenge of putting Brian's totally
demolished finger back together, almost as good as new. This was
another incident in the Applewood Farm saga, however, one
event after another continued to pile up, chipping away at my
resolve.

My inner voice coached me to be strong and keep the
frayed edges of my mind together. On an amazingly clear July day,
it promised to be hot with the humidity building as the day
progressed. A typical Maryland summer day. I cleaned up the
kitchen after breakfast, preparing to start the day's chores. The
phone rang.

"Brian can you get that?" I asked. He stood and picked up
the kitchen phone.

"Hi Dad, what's up?" Brian listened and then said, "Dad,
we've a lot to get done this weekend, but let me check with Pat.
Hold on." Putting his hand over the mouthpiece, Brian turned to
me and said, "Butch, Dad wants to know if we want to go out on
the boat for a few hours today ..."

In my typical, nose-to-the-grindstone attitude, I couched
my response, "Well, we've a whole list of stuff we need to do. You
know what that means if we go."

"Yeah! We work our asses off the rest of the week. We
never take time off. It's a beautiful day. The work will be here ... I
say we should do it," said Brian. He provided the perfect
counterpoint to my bring-on-the-guilt complex about having a
little fun. As I listened to myself, I knew I needed to get out of my
own way, but how to do it?

On the way to Gil's 26-foot Trojan named the *Southern
Mist*, we stopped to pick up Kentucky Fried Chicken, potato salad,
and coleslaw for lunch. We left Havre de Grace's Tidewater
Marina at the head of the Chesapeake Bay and motored down
and across to Tolchester on the eastern shore. The day's heat
coaxed us into the cool bay waters as soon as we helped Gil
anchor in a cove. Brian's Mom chose not to join us that particular

day and a calm atmosphere allowed us to unwind. We basked in the sun.

At about three o'clock Gil pointed to the western sky, "Looks like we've some hefty clouds building over there, and they look pretty threatening. I think we should pull up anchor and head back."

"Okay Dad. It's going to be late when we get back as it is, so let's go." Brian helped with the lines and the anchor, and I tidied up the galley.

Arriving back at the marina, we docked, loaded the car, and started the 20-mile drive back to Applewood. We saw indication of wet roads but no evidence of storm damage. We turned into our farm lane and saw signs of heavy rain. Deep ruts cut into the stone drive, created by the force of run-off. We knew then a strong storm must have moved through. Everything sparkled from the cleansing rain, and the humidity eased a bit.

As we walked down to the house, we saw heavy overspill from the fields above the house. Flattened grass and debris hinted at more. Siddy and Chrissy, our two golden retrievers, were down in the new basement and needed to be let out for a run. Whining emanated from behind the inside basement door. I opened the door and Siddy came charging out, Chrissy right behind, practically knocking me off my feet. Regaining my footing and looking to see what had the dogs so distraught, my mouth dropped. "Oh … my … God. Oh … my … God. Brian, come here, quick." I moved down the first three basement steps to get a better view. The dining table I'd been refinishing floated by. Assorted chairs followed suit. The landing for the steps was submerged, which meant that at least four feet of water filled our entire 40-by 18-foot basement.

Brian hollered from the other, outside, basement door, where an area had recently been excavated for steps, "Butch, the dirt walls collapsed and buried the sump pump. The water built up, and the pressure burst the door open. It's still pouring in. We need to figure out something before it hits the electrical box. Call the fire department: they have pumps. Tell them it's an emergency."

After making the call I looked at the rising, reddish, dirty water, pulling topsoil from our fields into our new basement. Despair flowed over me, mimicking the churning, swirling currents below. I don't remember much of the aftermath. I turned away and slowly climbed the stairs to the guest room. I lay down and curled into a fetal ball, my mind seeking a safe refuge away from the chaos below.

What were these sad, empty, and helpless feelings? Certainly they were foreign to peppy, positive me and very scary. Too embarrassed to give voice to what might be viewed as weak, I pulled myself together and forged ahead, as was expected, never considering professional counsel. Mom suffered from depression off and on over the years, but certainly no such malady applied to me. And surely a bad patch didn't constitute a condition. My husband was great, weren't we living our dream?

Moving On

It was time to get working on the second part of our marriage contract: raising a family. We spent serious effort on this particular endeavor, and we "did it" everywhere: in the dusty hay loft; on pine needles in the woods, interrupted by a trumpeting deer; on the new-mown lawn beneath twinkling stars; under the hot summer sun; and, of course, in our spacious king-sized bed. This was a year glorious in its intensity, effort, and fun, and it served to tamp down my feelings of inadequacy, even if they did float menacingly to the surface occasionally as the lack of results of our efforts felt frustratingly disappointing. At 33 my biological clock was tick-tick-ticking.

So began a series of doctors' appointments; tests; and regimented, unromantic attempts to accomplish the deed, to no avail. After two years, we decided adoption might be the best option. On a visit into Baltimore to see Brian's Grandpop Pete and Great Aunt Martha, we shared our decision with them. Wrinkled and hard of hearing, Aunt Martha did not mince words expressing serious concern about the prospect of adopting. Face screwed in conviction, she exclaimed, "No! You shouldn't consider adopting someone else's child. No! You never know what you'll get, and you can't ever let anyone know. And if you do it, which you shouldn't, you can *never* tell the child."

Aunt Martha, a lifelong spinster, made her living first as a seamstress and then managing the factory for which she worked. Against her counsel, we signed up with Catholic Charities for the long and costly process, determined to raise our child as a treasured choice. Aunt Martha's attitude about keeping an adoption secret flew in the face of my growing commitment to be open about what was happening in my life. Brian was in full agreement. My plan included creating an annual story of our child's life beginning with how the adoption came about ... when it finally did. Our social worker, Margaret, cautioned that the process could take up to four years but that many couples got pregnant along the way, so she advised us to keep trying.

It did, indeed, take four years. During the long wait, we worked our farm. I'd like to think that my Dad was pleased that one of his children pursued agriculture but if he was, he never expressed it to me. Money continued to be tight. As an alternative to cattle, we raised cash crops of corn, soybeans, green beans, and sweet peas that helped pay our debts.

Our cash flow was in a bad way, and while I searched for meaningful employment off the farm to help out it was hard to find. I collected unemployment, and that felt like failure. It did not help my self-esteem feeling like I was surely the only person reduced to such a low. Eventually, A personnel job working for the fleet management firm Peterson Howell and Heather (PHH) in Hunt Valley Industrial Park, located 30 miles from the farm, was offered and accepted. Working in the private sector proved an eye-opener and a lot to learn about life in the fast lane at PHH. If an employee didn't cooperate or play the game correctly, an escort out the door for little or no cause could be the result. Working in the personnel department would mean I sometimes performed the escorting.

My first day on the job, my department manager Mr. Jim Pursley took me to lunch in the company cafeteria and explained, "You see all these people around you, Pat? They're all good looking and young. PHH *only* hires young, good-looking employees, and the average age here is 32."

I felt intimidated and skeptical. I listened to Jim's words, realizing that a message lay hidden behind his grin. The work environment proved slippery and loose. During my first weeks on the job, many employees visited my office to check me out— mostly men used to getting what they wanted. Fleet management meant the company handled fleets of cars for other companies. As a result, they hired many former car salesmen. I was newly and happily married and had a hard time reconciling their casual attitude. Everyone seemed on the prowl. After-work parties were routine rather than an exception.

One particular encounter remains crystal clear in my memory. Assigned a small private office to conduct interviews of potential clerical staff, I busily applied myself, learning the ins and outs of PHH. One day I sensed a presence and looked up. In the doorway hovered Bob from logistics and supply.

"Hi, Bob," I said, "What can I do for you today?"

"Well, Pat, I just wanted to drop by and say hi … welcome you to PHH … you know, get acquainted." He edged around the corner of my desk, pinning me in the corner.

"Ooooookay, Bob. Let's see, you work, where? In which department?" I tried to buy myself time while I considered my options.

"In logistics, just across the hall. You know, Pat, I'm the head of that department and I've had my eye on you … thought maybe I could show you the ropes." He slunk closer.

"That's thoughtful of you, but Greta's a great supervisor and is teaching me what I need to know."

He leaned on the inside corner of my desk, inches away. "Pat, there are things about this company that I can teach you that will put you on the fast track."

Vaulting to my feet, panicky and stumbling, I stuck my right arm straight out, hand up, like a stop sign. "Look, Bob I'm doing just fine" I spoke with determination. "Now, if you'll please excuse me, I have to get back to work."

"Wellllllllll, you're not very grateful for my help," he protested, then pushed my arm aside and swooped in for a kiss. I pivoted, brought my right fist back, then forward landing it squarely in his gut. Let the record show that Bob was much taller than I: six feet to my five. He expelled a whoosh of air, looking shocked.

"Bob, I'm a happily married woman and have absolutely no interest in your help or intentions. It's time for you to leave, and don't come back."

He appeared as stunned as I. It felt good to stand my ground, speak with a firm true voice, and realize that even though Bob could make life difficult at work, a clear signal had been sent that I was not one of the party girls.

Speaking openly about being content in my marriage, made me stick out like a sour grape at PHH. I declined party invitations to get home to my husband and the farm. My attitude was considered quaint and bizarre to rising corporate executives. To survive in the job I was hired to do hard work was necessary. We really needed my income. Thankfully, my immediate supervisor, Greta Rose, was a savvy woman about my age, and we learned a lot from each other. She originated in the coalfields of West Virginia. Greta was street and business smart, recently divorced, with three boys born before she was nineteen. She protected me from prowling wolves, and recognized and rewarded my contributions to the organization.

Besides the less-than-ideal working conditions at PHH, there were other difficulties. By 1979 gas prices were escalating, and carpooling became the order of the day. I designed and implemented a carpool program for PHH, and participated with three other employees where we met in Bel Air for the daily drive to the office. In March of that year, the nuclear plant at Three Mile Island in Harrisburg, Pennsylvania, had a cooling system failure that led to the overheating and partial melting of its uranium core, raising fears of an explosion. Our farm lay 30 miles south of Three Mile Island, and PHH was 30 more miles beyond that. We all lived in a direct line of any potential fallout and exposure to radiation. Tension controlled the work environment, and little was accomplished during the 12 days it took officials to get a handle on the situation and return operations of the nuclear plant to normal. I hoped for a return to a routine in my job too, but it never came. I began a serious campaign to find another position, hopefully closer to the farm.

Four years at PHH and conditions for me continued to deteriorate. Those years were equally hard on Brian because many nights found me sobbing in his arms, railing against the injustices experienced, heard, and witnessed during my workday. Prior to our move to the farm, I interviewed with the Director of Personnel, Bill Foland, at Aberdeen Proving Ground (APG). The interview went well, and we reached a mutual understanding that he would have a job waiting for me when my six months of paid leave ran out. Mr. Foland liked the idea of having a CIA spook work for him. Unfortunately, Mr. Foland took a leave for knee surgery, and his designee didn't appreciate being told who to hire. Four years later, my office phone at PHH rang.

"Hello, PHH, Pat Adelhardt speaking. How can I help you?"

"Pat, it's Bill Foland from APG."

"Oh, my gosh. It's great to hear from you Mr. Foland."

"I was just going through my desk drawer and found your resume," he said enthusiastically. "Where're you, and why aren't you here?"

What a Godsend. I looked across my office with one eye looking out the door.

"I sure would like to be. I'm delighted you called. Tell me what I need to do." It took a few months to clear all the bureaucratic hurdles but APG swore me in on November 29, 1979. At last I had job security and a decent salary, two things found wanting at PHH.

Two years after starting my job at Aberdeen Proving Ground, a call came from the Equal Employment Opportunity Commission (EEOC) concerning a class action suit against PHH because of the prejudicial way they treated women. The EEOC representative made two visits to my office to persuade me to testify. She claimed that my testimony played a crucial role in their case and would provide the clout to finally bring PHH to heel, forcing the company to change its ways. I was reluctant to open old wounds, but knew it was right for me to speak out. Also, my personnel experience at PHH placed me in a unique position to give credible testimony. In the early 1980s women began to gain a voice, and I had become more practiced in sharing my own.

The Class Action Suit against PHH prevailed, and positive changes took effect to the benefit of every woman still employed there.

During all of this, Brian held a string of jobs but never found the right fit. Finally, a budget officer position opened at the Whiteford Packing Company, a local frozen food processing plant just five miles from the farm, and it proved suitable for the time being. Brian applied his farming and educational skills and learned management and budget proficiencies at the same time. At last we were both employed with solid jobs and could focus on our goal of building a family.

We remained in regular contact with Margaret, our Catholic Charities social worker, and completed all the interviews and physicals. Only the home study remained to complete our adoption process and we'd been told it took six months after that for a couple to learn if a newborn baby was ready for placement. Consequently, we purposely put off fixing a baby's room or picking a name knowing we'd have ample time.

One July day in 1980, Margaret called Brian at the packing company. "Brian, are you and Pat still interested in adopting?"

"Yes, Margaret, of course we are. You're calling about a date for the home study, right?"

"We'll get to that. But first … I've got your baby!" she exclaimed.

After a stunned pause, Brian blurted, "My God! But we haven't done the home study, Margaret."

"Oh, we'll get to that," she said.

"This is great news! Is it a girl or boy?" Brian asked.

"It's a boy, born on May 31st, five weeks premature. He's just been released from the hospital and is with foster parents who work for us, Mr. and Mrs. Gifford. We'll get the home study done quickly, and then he's yours."

"Wow! I don't know what to say! This is great!"

"His mother, a 19-year-old Catholic woman of Italian, French and Polish descent is not in a position to care for her baby," Margaret explained. "The father is of Italian descent and skipped town once he heard of the mother's pregnancy. She desires her baby to be the adopting family's first child. She wants him reared in a rural environment, preferably on a farm, and also raised Catholic. Sounds like a match made in heaven to me. Since you and Pat fit the bill perfectly, we'll expedite everything from here," Margaret said.

"Let me call Pat and get back to you by the end of the day, okay?" said Brian, full of excitement. He called me at APG right away. "Butch, are you in the middle of something? Can you talk?"

"Sure, it's okay. What's up?"

"Butch, I just talked to Margaret from Catholic Charities," Brian said eagerly. "She has our baby, and it's a boy."

Stunned into silence, alarm rose to the fore. I whispered meekly, "I can't believe it. What about the home study? She told us it'd be months after the home study before we'd be notified. My God. I can't believe it's happening. Tell me what she said."

Brian shared everything he knew with growing excitement. "I think we should tell Margaret we can take him as soon as we can get the little guy, don't you?"

"Let's think about this a minute," I said. "No question, it's the very best news. But—we haven't fixed a baby's room or even picked a name, we've no baby clothes, no diapers, nothing." My voice quivered. How could I be unprepared after six years of waiting? I'm going to be a mother for real, and they want me to be one right now. Could I do the job right? I wanted to be a different parent in many ways from what I experienced and witnessed growing up: no to black straps, silent treatments, and sarcasm: yes to encouragement, love, and peace in our home.

"Butchie, it's going to be all right, trust me. I'll call Margaret and tell her we'll let her know tomorrow. We'll take a walk and talk about it when we get home tonight, okay?

I sat at my desk, dazed by the news. Our longed-for dream could become reality within two days. Chaos ruled In my mind. Since I was a young girl, I'd had a penchant for organizing: people, things, places—not to excess, but the habit definitely marked me, an innate character trait. When the neighborhood kids needed an activity like cops and robbers, cowboys and Indians, or a good snowball fight, I usually assigned the places, roles, and rules of the game. This pattern continued through high school where I spearheaded political campaigns for friends who ran for school offices and chaired the calendar drive to raise money for events. Always a planner, paired with a vision of how things come to fruition. The reality of our baby already born, possibly in our home at the farm, threw me for a loop. The need to stop and breathe, to take it in, to make things ready and pick a name, overcame me. Envisioning a quiet time with Brian after work to sort things out was a comfort.

Strolling with Brian through the tender green ferns of our asparagus patch, my insecurity surfaced. "I'm scared. I don't know the first thing about being a mother, changing a diaper, feeding..."

"You'll be a natural, Butch. We can put him in a dresser drawer," he laughed assuredly. "We'll get organized. You'll see. It will work."

"What will we call him? We haven't even talked about that," I said, near tears. "Brian, I need some time," I pleaded. "Margaret told you he was premature and had just been released from the hospital to his foster parents, right? Can I have a week? Besides marrying you, this is the next most important thing I'll ever do in my life. I want to savor it. I want to be ready." Seeing my fear and understanding this basic need of mine, Brian agreed.

In retrospect, I often wonder what was the worst thing that could have happened? I would have done fine, risen to the occasion as always. Rationally, as I reflect, I know I made the right decision for me, enabling me to parent from day one the best that I knew how. Still, the guilt of waiting those extra 10 days picks and scrapes my subconscious.

There was much to attend to at work to ensure that I had a position in which to return after four months of maternity leave. Fortunately, Bill Foland believed the work I had done in starting and managing the Disability Program for the installation made an impact, and he wanted it continued. Ed Stubbs, my division chief, had unceremoniously dumped the program on my desk the year before. It was an unwanted stepchild no one chose to touch. I suspected Ed secretly hoped I would fail because he repeatedly criticized my efforts to launch the program that was intended to secure jobs on the installation for disabled applicants. I took it as a chance to prove myself and gain the possible opportunity to return part-time once our adoption came through. I met and consulted with Bill prior to departing on leave.

"Pat, you've made a real mark with this program in the short time you've been here," he said. "Surprising, since you didn't know anything about how the Army works when you started. But I figured a former CIA agent could manage. I think you'd make a contribution no matter how often you're in the office. So you're wanting to come back only part time after your maternity leave. How many days do you want to work?"

"I'd like to work two days a week as a permanent part-timer with the option of adding days in the future" I replied hopefully.

"Are you aware the installation doesn't have permanent part-timers? We usually only keep them on as temporaries."

"I've heard that, Bill, but you need to start somewhere, and I promise you, I'll not disappoint, if you take a chance on me. I need the benefits." I held my breath. I'd revealed what I needed most for my family and me. Now it was up to him.

"Ed is not going to like this ... Okay, you need to write up a memo stating your request with the days of the week you want to work and send it through Ed to me. I'll approve it, even though he'll give me an argument. You know he didn't like the fact I made him hire you in the first place," said Bill with a grin.

Much to Ed's chagrin, I began maternity leave with a sense of security and relief. I knew full well when I returned in November 1980, that Ed might make my working life miserable, but I didn't care. I felt confident in standing up for myself. I would find the fortitude to handle Ed.

Small Package

The days before Bryce Patrick Adelhardt came home filled us with fierce anticipation and humbling fear. We worried we would not be up to the job. At the same time, we wanted a baby more than anything imaginable. Together we could do anything, right? I mean we were college graduates and widely traveled to boot, so of course, surely, we could do this.

We scrubbed, peeled, scraped, and painted his room, everything happening double-time. I met with Dr. Arnie Lavenstein, a pediatrician, to learn the ropes of feeding and a baby's medical needs. Shopping and collecting the basics in bedding, diapers, clothing, toys, car seat, high chair—everything cute and adorable. Once completed, Bryce's room looked picture-perfect and included a piece of Adelhardt memorabilia. A worn oak table was resurrected as a changing table. In its former life it served as an operating table where Grandpop Gil lay to have his tonsils removed. We resurrected the wooden crib; well worn by three Adelhardt babies, and added a colorful mobile to tinkle above. Farm animal watercolors of a pig, lamb, cow, chicken, and horse hung on the wall above his crib to complete the decorations.

July 11th dawned with an already hot sun, a damp haze of humidity hung over the fields. Anticipation charged the air. We would pick up our son at the Stella Maris, St. Vincent's orphanage north of Baltimore in the early afternoon. Brian and I raced around, tense and rattled. Studying my to-do list, we worked together to make sure every last thing received a checkmark before we hauled the diaper bag, car seat, and our properly dressed selves (Brian in coat and tie, and I in a cotton dress and heels) to the car. Finally, we were ready to drive to St. Vincent's. We allowed ample time, and I figured we would end up waiting in the parking lot until the appointed hour. "Butch, I need to stop by

184

Harford Mall in Bel Air for a minute on the way, okay?" Brian said and seemed to be holding the wheel for dear life.

"What in heaven's sake for? Did we forget something?" I asked.

"Well, I need to get something for Bryce. I saw it advertised on TV this week ... It's a teddy bear with a recording of the sounds made while the baby is still in the womb. Don't you think that'd be comforting?"

"That's a great idea, but do we really have time? You know what a zoo Harford Mall can be." As I talked, I touched his arm, a wave of love and affection welling within. Tears escaped. I felt blessed, married to a man who possessed such tenderness and the emotional strength to express it.

"We'll make time. He has to have that teddy bear to soothe him. Think of what he's already been through in his young life: taken from his birth mother, rejected by his father, living with foster parents for these few weeks and now, ending up with two people who don't know what they're doing." He laughed, looking as emotional and tense as I.

Even with the unplanned stop, we arrived on time. Sister Ann Marie ushered us into a hushed room, advising, "You two take a minute to catch your breath. Your son and his foster parents, Mr. and Mrs. Gifford, will be here in a few minutes."

In they came, bearing our greatest gift. Bryce weighed 5 pounds 6 ounces and was only 19 inches long, very tiny for being six-weeks old. Mrs. Gifford expertly transferred Bryce from his car-seat carrier into my tentative arms.

"Oh, my! How beautiful you are, Bryce Patrick," I said as tears welled again. I examined our treasure beyond measure in his tiny blue-and-brown striped top and shorts, booties covering his toes, eyes so blue the sky could not compare, and a tuft of dark brown hair crowning his flawlessly shaped head. I was in love. I passed Bryce to his Dad, and he seemed to disappear into Brian's large hands. Tenderness welled at the realization of our dream.

Before departing, the Giffords shared with us that they returned from a camping trip with Bryce the week before (unimaginable to me), and to expect a lot of grunting, tooting, and smiling as he lightly slept. Sister Ann Marie escorted the three of us, the new Adelhardt Family, into the chapel and performed a blessing for our success and prosperity, then sent us on our way.

In the parking lot, we tackled the car seat for the first time, trying not to strangle our son in the process. Once secure, Brian gently presented his son with the teddy bear. He turned on the soothing amniotic sounds in its tummy, and off we went toward Applewood Farm with a quick stop on the way to introduce Bryce to his grandparents. Gil and Eileen became a reliable source of baby-rearing information and comfort as we launched into this new journey.

The twenty miles from Gil and Eileen's house seemed endless and as we drove down our lane, my feelings of inadequacy intensified. We really were on our own with this tot; he was totally dependent on us to raise him. I was desperate not to repeat the errors my own parents had made. As we drew in front of the house, we noticed a huge sign: "Welcome Home Bryce Patrick Adelhardt!"

"Oh, no! What's this—oh, how nice! I bet Betsy did that," I said. Betsy and Dick Fleischman, our closest neighbors around our age, had befriended us since our move to the farm. We walked down to the house, baby and teddy bear in my arms. Brian opened the door and with a sigh of relief I was ready to start my "new mother" role in privacy.

An explosion of sound enveloped us. "Surprise! Congratulations! Oh, let us see," chorused family, friends, and neighbors. Gil and Eileen brought up the rear, having followed us discreetly up the road. Bryce quickly let everyone know how he felt about the proceedings, letting loose an enormous poop that oozed out of his diaper, onto my arms, and down my dress. That stink transformed the room! Grandma Eileen thrilled at the opportunity to whisk Bryce to the changing table and swap his

186

diaper as I, the rattled Mom, escaped to the upstairs shower to regain my composure.

I can still feel the steady stream of water hitting my body, ridding myself of new baby poop, shaking with tension as I reviewed the last few hours. *Well, Patricia, you're a mother now, and that beautiful child is counting on you to act like one. You can't hide in this shower all afternoon and relinquish that precious gift to Eileen.* That did it. Calming myself, I rejoined the party, tugged my son from his grandmother's reluctant arms and assumed my rightful role.

Those first four months with Bryce were magical for us, but especially for me, since I spent every moment with him while on maternity leave from the office. To this day I'm thankful I persisted.

Working part-time was the right choice for our growing family, but it contributed to the recurring struggle to meet our financial obligations.

Brian, came home from work one day that August looking quite desperate.

"Did you have a good day?" I asked. I turned and studied his drawn face. "Brian what's the matter? You look like you've lost your best friend."

"Butch, let's put Bryce in his snuggly and take a walk around the farm." A stroll through the fields helped anchor us, a common practice we adopted.

Past the barn stood the withering fields of crops: corn stunted and brown, soybeans drooping. These sights pierced my soul. With no rain since the spring planting, the Maryland sun was ravaging our crops. Walking through the meadow to the top of "our" hill, we surveyed the gently rolling fields. From here, most things of any import could be hashed out.

Brian tentatively began, "Butch our crops have failed and I don't know what to do. This heat is bad enough, but no rain— nothing we planted in the spring will make it; it's all shriveling up.

You saw how it looked just now." I listened and heard the desperation in Brian's voice. I knew we were at a crossroads.

"I know. How will we pay our mortgage and this year's operating expenses?" I asked. Our mortgage was paid in a lump sum annually, and the deadline loomed.

"Not only that, but the operating loan is coming due at the same time, and right now I don't have a clue as to how we're going to get out of this one. I was thinking maybe we should sell a piece off the farm, like the back corner. What do you think?"

I pondered silently. I sensed the misery of defeat, of losing what we worked hard to achieve.

"No." I looked Brian in the eye; my hand resting on Bryce's silken curls. I spoke slowly, deliberately, emphatically, testing each word. I trusted God to help me find the right words. "I think, Brian ... that selling a piece of our farm—or all of it—is not an option. We must find another way. We've a few months to figure it out. Do you think the good Lord led us here, sent us Bryce, and then intended for us to quit? I don't think so. We'll find another way." Brian's face lit with a relieved smile. We turned for home, united with new determination, and the setting sun cast a golden mantle of hope.

Filled with new resolve, Brian approached our FHA loan officer. FHA encouraged farmers to take big loans for farm improvements and operating expenses. Brian felt confident that he and Bill would find a solution.

Bill welcomed Brian into his office, but the meeting began on a less than auspicious note as Bill said, "There's been a change in policy this year, Brian. In fact, you were on my list of farmers to call this week. Not only can I not loan you more money, but if you don't come up with what you owe FHA by December 31st, we're going to foreclose."

I imagine the blood drained from Brian's face. Stark reality dawned. "Bill! I can't believe this. For six years, you've been shoving money at me like it came from a bottomless pit. Now, out of the blue, you're telling me you're going to foreclose?"

Dejected and discouraged, Brian went to the local feed mill, Service Feed and Supply, where we kept a running tab for seed, fertilizer, and chemicals. Brian valued the advice of the owner, Marlyn, who started his business from scratch much like we had. Marlyn was rough around the edges, and a constant tease, but his business sense usually proved sound. Swallowing his pride, Brian explained our dilemma.

"Brian, don't sell real estate no matter what you do. You'd regret it, and so would I. How long have you and Pat been on the farm now?"

"Six years, last April. Why?"

"You've built up equity those six years. That's a chip to go to the bank with and see if they'll loan you money to pay your mortgage and operating loans," Marlyn advised.

"Marlyn, I owe you too. Even more than what we owe FHA."

"Brian, I'll work with you. You can pay me a little at a time."

Brian thanked Marlyn for his advice and generosity and left more confident.

As Brian related the events of the day over dinner that night, hope glimmered. Tension eased a little, and I prayed harder that a way to save the farm would materialize. I anguished over whether I had pushed Brian too far, since most of the burden for coming up with a solution rested on his shoulders.

"Brian, I think you've a good chance of success with the bank. You know how to talk to those folks," I said.

"I think you're right about not selling even a piece of the farm, but I didn't—couldn't—see another way. Now it looks like we might have some options. We'll take it a day at a time and hope for the best. I realize we've a partnership with the Man upstairs, and I need to stay tuned." Brian spoke confidently.

Brian's boss at Whiteford Packing Company enjoyed connections with a local bank manager, who turned out to be accommodating and encouraging. An appraisal of the farm would determine whether the bank could loan us money. That process produced anxious days and sleepless nights. We waited. Appraisal complete, the bank discovered the farm's worth now exceeded what we paid for it. We possessed equity, a brand-new bargaining tool and the ticket to a brighter future. The bank happily loaned us the money.

Applewood Farm faced a pivotal year in1980. We knew with certainty, God put Marlyn in our path at the right time. Together, we could do anything—with help from above.

Baby Bryce continued to satisfy my every need to mother. I filled to the brim with a deep love. Every day, he performed some new, extraordinary feat: smiling so sweet it made me cry, sleeping serenely as only *our* child could. Every part of his little body intrigued and fascinated me, from his perfectly formed toes and fingers to his smooth, adorable, and kissable bottom. Bath time became a special treat once I got my nerves under control. Bryce was so tiny, I feared drowning him. I started out using a small Rubbermaid basin. He splashed and gurgled with glee, and my heart swelled with joy at God's perfect creation.

We celebrated Bryce's first birthday on May 31, 1981, with a crab feed. As much of the family as we could gather came for the Maryland delicacy, picking hard blue crabs, fresh from the Chesapeake Bay. Special guests included Aunt Dorothy and Uncle Jonsie, who drove from Arlington, Virginia, bringing a uniquely designed, home-baked birthday cake for the occasion ... a tradition that continued as Bryce grew older. Each year Dorothy out-did herself with birthday cakes. Designs and shapes ranged from a farm tractor, a car, a circus scene, and a cowboy with a lariat, to name a few. The cake, always carefully crafted, was transported on blocks of ice for the two-hour trip. Saved till last, this confectionery became the piecé de résistance of our annual spring birthday celebration.

The eight or nine dozen large, live, blue male crabs came in a bushel basket. Long steel tongs in hand, Brian wrestled each crab into the speckled cooking kettle that was waiting in the sink.

We raced to capture those that skittered down the sides and across the kitchen floor without getting our fingers pinched. The agitated crabs clicked their claws and spewed tiny bubbles. Brian weighted down the lid with a cast iron skillet to prevent escapees as the heat increased and the rat-a-tat-tat on the kettle lid reached a crescendo. The crabs quieted and steamed in Old Bay spices, dry yellow mustard, pepper, and vinegar, rosy red and seasoned to perfection. Aromas wafting from that crab kettle can bring a Marylander to his or her knees in anticipation of the coming feast. Brian and I set up a long table on the screened porch covering it with newspaper thick enough to absorb the crab juices, pounding crab mallets, and bits of shell.

In the early days, Bryce always sat next to his Grandma Adelhardt so she could school him in the art of crab picking. She was a difficult woman under the best of circumstances, but place her at a table piled high with crabs and she purred like a kitten.

"Bryce, just look at what I have for you!" Grandma Adelhardt often crooned, holding up a juicy lump of crab. "It's the lollypop, the best part of the crab. You eat it just like you'd bite a sucker." The perfectly cracked claw wobbled in the air. Bryce grasped the delicacy in his tiny mitt and did as instructed, sucking and chomping with a look of pure pleasure.

It was a long slow process, that crab picking. Time eddied, conversation was leisurely. Mallets banged the table, juice and fat flying. Mellow beer, fried chicken, potato salad, deviled eggs and that homemade birthday cake with ice cream topped everything off, ushering in the beginning of summer.

Child-Rearing

As Bryce grew, he became part of everything—on and off the farm. When he was a toddler, he participated in the spring Christmas tree plantings in mid-March, when the soil was moist, the air brisk and damp. This process evolved over the years from hand planting to renting a tree planter from the Forest Service. The tree planter was much easier on all of us and enabled little Bryce to come along. Grandpop Gil drove the tractor. Bryce and I dressed in rubber overalls, boots, and gloves. I sat on the tree planter's hard cold metal seat as it knifed through the earth. I straddled the holes, spaced at six-foot intervals, that waited to receive the tiny seedling I held in my hand. Gurgling happily in one of the metal rectangular planter bins, Bryce spent the day accompanying me.

On the planter next to Bryce, Brian kept the three other tree bins filled with root-trimmed and moistened seedlings. In two to three long days, depending on the conditions, the task was done. By day's end we were weary, wet, and mud-splattered. As our Christmas tree sales grew, we planted as many as ten thousand seedlings during that spring ritual, spurred to build Bryce's college fund.

Wondering if it was unfair to Bryce, subjecting him to long days out in the elements, I remembered working in our Oregon orchards from a young age, but never whole days as a toddler. Looking back, it was clear my parents instilled a strong work ethic in me, and my resentment of them had been replaced by gratitude. I also recognized that following Dad's attempt to make time in the workday for fun had merit, whether it was a midmorning break from thinning apples to watching 30 minutes of a political convention to letting us escape to Kobergs Beach on the Columbia River to swim and frolic. Becoming a mother gave me new insight into the ways I had been parented. Pushing through a barrier of blame, I accepted my parents as they were:

two people who did the best they knew how. My upbringing could now be viewed in a new light. Taking the good and leaving the rest behind was my goal.

In late September each year, we took a trip to Hershey Park, an amusement center an hour and a half from the farm. Over the years, Bryce took his greatest pleasure in riding the three roller coasters. He challenged his dad to join him on the Super Dooper Looper but it took Brian two years of studying the daunting ride before he accepted the dare. Both pumped up with excitement, they started in on me, trying, unsuccessfully to convince me that it was nothing of which to be scared.

Limited time existed for other recreation in those years, so we took our pleasure in long walks around the farm, enjoying the cast of late afternoon shadows across gentle slopes. Brian and I treasured these moments as we squatted on our favorite hill to plan, dream, and sort the problems of the day. Bryce and the dogs scampered around us. As evenings drew near in summer, the fields lit with a dusting of fireflies. Soon, they danced in a full twinkling chorus, lighting the deepening night. Bullfrogs added their deep croaks, and cicadas clattered ballads that waxed and waned through the evening.

Downward Spiral

In the mid-1980s, an opportunity came our way to purchase a sailing school and boat charter business. It seemed like a nice fit with our farm operation, because the bulk of work fell during the summer. For 10 years we owned and operated Havre de Grace Sailing School and Charter along with the farm. However, running two businesses—not to mention my part-time job in personnel with the U.S. Army and raising Bryce, now a pre-teenager—swallowed us whole.

Sailing was one of our favorite pastimes, but the reality hit us hard: once we owned a sailing business, we had little time to actually sail. Brian knew it was time to call it quits the day one of our charter sailboats caught its mast between the train rails of the Havre de Grace Railroad Bridge. This particular bridge connected the entire rail system on the eastern seaboard. The next Amtrak train was due to cross the bridge within the hour. Disaster was narrowly averted. The stress and tension of those harrowing moments left an indelible mark on Brian.

After this calamitous event, a fateful window of opportunity delivered Brian the chance to serve upon the nonprofit, educational vessel *Martha Lewis*. This possibility struck a harmonious cord in Brian, connecting him to the saltwater roots of his ancestors. His grandparents and uncles had worked as oyster dredgers on the Eastern Shore of Maryland for decades. Brian and his parents visited them often, and Brian remembered the thrill of riding along as his uncles dredged the abundant bay waters.

As a licensed captain, who sailed the bay since high school, Brian was eminently qualified to run the Martha Lewis. He felt this offer satisfied many fronts: the sailing school and charter business could be sold; the job would provide a small but steady income; he could teach junior and high school students about the

Chesapeake Bay; and the work would provide a challenge to learn the ins and outs of sailing an oyster dredge.

Brian took the job as Captain. I did not have a good feeling about this abrupt change, but Brian's positive outlook prevailed. Off he sailed on another new adventure, and he was gone—a lot. Bryce and I were left to fend for ourselves, and we found ourselves battling the intruding black snake, which had taken up a brief residence under our dining table. This ominous intruder mirrored my frame of mind.

In addition to my own inner turmoil at this time, I faced my mother's misplaced anger and resentment toward me. Since Dad's death, I noticed an eroding of the close relationship we enjoyed. I attempted to understand what disconnected us as I followed the tenuous string of memories.

Dad had been diagnosed and treated with radiation for prostate cancer 10 years before. The doctors promised him 10 good years, which he got, but then the cancer spread into his bones. Up until that happened, he lived a full life working the orchard but his last year was a difficult one, filled with doctor visits, blood transfusions, and considerable pain. It was especially hard on Mom, although she cared for Dad without complaint.

Pete, my brother, lived in Oregon in the early 1980s while we girls all lived in the East. To give Mom some relief, we came up with a rotating schedule to fly to Oregon at different times during that last year. Maureen managed to take the longest stint during the fall harvest. She had been helping with the pear harvest for several consecutive years, so Dad knew he could depend on her. Ellen and I managed a week each. During my stay, I interviewed caregivers and tried to identify services to help Mom. Unfortunately, services for the elderly were limited, and hospice was nonexistent in Hood River.

A caregiver who agreed to an interview was located and Ellen Davis, one of the neighbors, agreed to come and stay with Dad under the guise of "just dropping by for a visit." Dad really liked Ellen, found her intelligent and witty, and enjoyed her company—or so I thought. When Mom and I returned home, Dad was adamant that he didn't want any "damn babysitter" because he could take care of himself.

"Dad, your doctor told me not to leave you alone."

"I don't care what the doctor said, I don't want it." He grouched.

"A caregiver occasionally would allow for Mom to get out once in awhile to run errands."

"Well, we'll see." Perhaps a small concession.

When my visit drew to a close, Ellen agreed to drive me to the Portland Airport for my early morning flight. As I prepared to leave, Mom expressed her gratitude and hugged me warmly. We shed a lot of tears during the week, shared many laughs and felt very close. On the day of my departure, as I was getting up, Dad came into the guest room to thank me for coming and to say goodbye. We embraced, and I hope, through my tears, I told him I loved him.

Dad died in the hospital in late September with Pete at his side, where he had shared the watch with Mom during Dad's last days. It was a difficult vigil, and I was grateful Pete was there.

After Dad's funeral as things quieted, the closeness that Mom and I shared made her pulling away all the more puzzling. One particular instance occurred when Brian, Bryce and I were visiting in Oregon. Generally, Mom was easygoing, but she did have a tendency to let things that irritated her build to a crescendo and then explode over something that seemed of little consequence. This time we were washing up after dinner, and somehow the subject of cleaning silver came up.

"Maureen gave a big soup-and-dessert party this past February for 25 friends," I said. "I helped her polish the sterling silver flatware so she could use it for that evening."

Like the stillness on water before a storm, Mom turned to me with a withering look. Then with the force of a teakettle coming to full boil, she exploded, "You've never once offered to polish my silver."

Mom's anger was so palpable and out of context for the easy conversation we were enjoying that I felt like I'd been slapped.

A couple of years later, I sought the help of a therapist to attempt to sort out why I was despondent. My therapist, Rita, and I spent time plying the murky depths of my subconscious and shed light on how and why this disconnect with Mom happened.

"Pat, I know you've thought about this situation with your Mom since we last met. Did you come to any conclusions?" Rita asked.

"I'm not sure it makes sense, Rita, but of her four children, I think Mom sees me as being the most like Dad."

"Okay. That's a start. What else?" Rita prodded.

"Well, I think Mom's still angry at him, but he's not here and I am. So, could she have transferred those feelings to me? It sure feels like it."

"Pat, good insight, nice work. I think you've come very close to hitting the nail on the head. I want you to consider having a conversation with your Mom about this."

"Oh my, Rita. That would be hard. I don't know if I can do it," I said as my stomach clenched.

"Well, having that conversation with your Mom in person will go a long way toward healing. Based on how you described what happened, I don't think your Mom realizes how she hurt you. Give it some thought. We can talk about it again on a later visit."

After letting Rita's suggestion percolate for a few weeks, I became more comfortable with the idea of having a talk with Mom about the situation. I saw no other way to prick this negative balloon and clarify the feelings swirling within.

Mom came east that fall for a visit, and although I trembled at the thought of broaching this sensitive subject with her, I gathered my courage during a walk one clear, sunny day.

I began, "Mom, you know I've been seeing a therapist for the past few months, right?"

"Yes, and I hope it's helping you," she said.

"It is, I think. Her name is Rita and in our sessions, she suggested that you and I talk about our relationship and how I feel it has changed since Dad died." My hands were clammy, my heart beating *a rat-a-tat-tat*, but I plunged on, explaining the situation, how it felt, and how I thought it had impaired our bond. As Mom's face transformed from puzzlement to realization, it looked like a light bulb being lit.

Hugging me hard, Mom said tearfully, "Pat, I didn't realize I was doing that to you, but I think you're right—it's probably true." From that day forward our relationship blossomed and remained strong.

Keeping hurt feelings and secrets had been a way of life for so many years. Sessions with Rita opened a new door for me, helping me see the connection between my bouts of depression and the implicit requirement to keep our family secrets tightly under wraps.

Facing and dealing with what I had repressed for more than 20 years strengthened my relationships and me. Brian and I formed a greater bond as well when I faced my fear of never being enough for him and of being too old for him. Rita encouraged that conversation as well, but embarking on that path was scarier than my talk with Mom. In fact, once I opened up to Brian, his approach to all things I held deep and dark was to help shine a light, easing the need for avoidance. I forged ahead toward freedom, anxious to be done with that dark season in my life.

Agri-Tourism

Once the Christmas trees were large enough to sell, we put out our "Choose and Cut" shingle and greeted customers from our front porch, presenting them with directions and a saw. As the years progressed, Christmas preparations started at Applewood Farm by November 1st each year. Eventually, we cleaned out the upper barn and made it the center of our operations.

During those first three weeks in November I decorated the barn, turning it into a winter wonderland with lights and greenery in every nook and cranny. Our goal was to make children and adults alike pop with excitement as they entered the barn. It was Brian's idea to string large maple branches with colored lights and then secure them in the eves of the barn. He also created two elevated train displays that produced equal squeals of delight.

We hired high school kids, many of them friends of Bryce, to help us decorate and later to sell the trees. It was fun training and working alongside these young people. Applewood Farm was a first job for most of them. I took seriously the responsibility of starting them in the working world realizing from my experiences in personnel that workers didn't automatically or innately know and understand what was expected. Brian and I impressed upon them that they represented the "face" of Applewood, and we worked to instill good habits in them from the beginning. We hired mostly honor students and they caught on quickly, and we have maintained lasting friendships with many.

When Bryce could reach the pedals and shift the gears of most of the farm equipment he was able to operate our small John Deere tractor and wagon to meet our customers as they cut their Christmas trees. At ten he was too young for a driver's license, but that rule didn't apply for farm equipment used strictly on the farm. Bryce tagged cut trees and brought them back to the barn for baling, a crucial but stressful part of the operation. Bryce

199

was conscious of keeping the customers content and making sure they didn't have to wait long for their tree. His sense of humor kept cheer in the holiday atmosphere.

Those days, I made and decorated a hundred wreaths out of cull trees—a misshapen or stunted tree—requiring late nights in the unheated barn. Over time, I realized I was resourceful and somewhat artistic, but there were moments when I'd ask myself, *Why am I doing this?* The answer came down to two things: First, the creative process of making and decorating the wreaths, barn, and trees was enjoyable. Second, it helped our bottom line. But beyond that, most of the time we were having fun making our vision come true.

Together, we shouldered the bumps in the road. One such bump came in 2005. One of the most popular days at the farm was when Santa and Mrs. Claus arrived in horse-drawn carriage, driven by our friend Jen and pulled by our faithful horse Big. Santa and Mrs. Claus—our long-time friends, Donny and Priscilla Forsythe, loved doing this ... at least up until we nearly did Donny in.

As was typical, parents and children came early and rushed to the barn to watch for Santa's arrival down the long lane. I was monitoring the crowd in the barn when Brian rushed in. He grabbed my elbow and whispered, "Butch I think I just killed Santa in front of 200 kids! Get some towels to dry him off. He seems okay, but he took a flying leap off the back of the carriage!"

"What? How?" I asked.

"When I asked Big to take one more step forward, the carriage jerked and Santa landed in that snowy-muddy glop."

After arriving at the barn entrance that day Donny assured me he was fine, as any seasoned actor would. He was a little muddy, but none the worse for wear. Despite the mishap, Santa and Mrs. Claus worked their magic on the crowd. We made slow progress through the crowd as I escorted them to a special spot in the barn where they could listen to all the kids' Christmas wishes while parents took pictures. I watched Santa laugh with glee and grab his belly, and I acknowledged even then it would be a lasting memory.

Our animals played a significant role in creating farm memories too and were a popular attraction to our operation. All of them worked for their keep, which helped the balance sheet. That is why when one day Brian said, "Butch, I've been looking into the possibility of buying a small reindeer herd," I was somewhat receptive. It was the fall Bryce departed for his first year of college and we both were suffering with empty nest syndrome. Maybe an addition to our animal family would help.

"Really? Isn't that going to be expensive?" I asked. "Don't they have to come all the way from Alaska?"

"Yes, they do. It costs some bucks, but it'd be an investment. It'd also be a farm expense that'd reduce our taxes," he said. Brian knew that if he could show how the outlay would positively impact our bottom line, he had a good chance of winning me over.

And so, a small reindeer herd arrived at the farm that fall. The herd included a bull we named Spruce, because even for a yearling he stood tall and sturdy like an evergreen, and three doe-eyed females named Serena, Comet, and Sassy (out of respect for their evolving personalities). One evening we sat in the corral, watching their reindeer antics. The pen Brian built gave them plenty of running room. They got going so fast they seemed to fly. Smiling, I confessed, "You know, Brian I have to hand it to you. These guys aren't only gregarious and sweet, but they're hysterical to watch. Our customers are going to love them."

"You think?" replied Brian. "It's nice to hear you're feeling better about our buying them."

"Yep, I am. And I'll enjoy marketing them for our Christmas season. I predict we, or I should say *they*, will draw record crowds to our farm." I felt somewhat mollified since I was rather reluctant about buying the reindeer. I now envisioned our bottom line turning from red to black. This experience made me realize that once I got past the risk, like buying reindeer, my adrenalin put me in drive and my creative juices took off.

Reindeer at Christmas generated free press. The key word here is "free." The sole reason for this unexpected gift? The "girls," as we affectionately called the reindeer. The females participated in the educational talks Brian gave during the Christmas season, but Spruce was usually in rut at that time which made him not very sociable and a bit too frisky to be around crowds. Print media, radio, and TV all wanted to showcase our unique attraction. As the saying goes, *build it and they will come*— and they did, in the hundreds that first year and in the thousands as the years progressed.

Treasured memories developed with additions to our petting zoo, even though they usually created some angst in me. Brian's love for all animals ran counter to my need to keep our books balanced. One September such an addition appeared. Arriving home from my job at the Aberdeen Proving Ground I noticed a weird noise as I exited my car. It seemed to be coming from the barn. Brian came out of the house laughing, eyes twinkling.

"Brian, what's that noise going on in the barn?" I asked.

"Come on, you've got to see this." He radiated excitement. There stood a tiny four-legged thing, no bigger than a fuzzy stuffed animal desperate for hugs. Brian explained she was a miniature Sicilian burro just weaned, exactly like the one that pregnant Mary rode to Bethlehem. Each Sicilian burro bore a symbolic cross on its back. The one in our barn was so teeny she arrived at the farm in the backseat of our white jeep Cherokee, her head over Brian's shoulder. Brian bought her as a surprise for me, so he said, but I think he fell in love with her and couldn't bear not to bring her home. While small in stature, she made up for it with her big voice.

We named her Sophina, Sophie for short. Sophie immediately imprinted on Brian since she missed her mother.

Another mouth to feed, I thought. I consoled myself knowing she would win people's hearts, making her a financial asset.

In 1999, shortly after Sophie's arrival, we felt we could finally realize our dream of Brian working full-time on the farm, as long as I continued to work my job at Aberdeen Proving Ground. To solidify our decision and bottom line, Brian decided to grow pumpkins to add five weeks and another season of being open to the public. From that point on, we opened the farm with Fallfest, our version of a festival with music, vendors, magicians, puppeteers, and the farm's permanent fall displays. As we prepared to open the gates for the first time, working frantically to finish last-minute things, I heard Brian shout to me from across the field, "Butch, have you seen Sophie?"

"No. What do you mean, have I seen her? We're getting ready to open in an hour."

"I can't find her anywhere. I'm going to jump in the Jeep, and try to figure out where she's gone."

"Okay, but hurry," I hollered from the barn.

We didn't have much fencing on the farm in those days but we always thought the animals stayed close ... until we discovered otherwise. Brian went looking. Quizzing all the neighbors he heard, "Oh sure, Brian, we see your dog BJ and that cute little burro almost every day. They've a regular route they travel together. BJ's always in the lead."

Finally, Brian came upon BJ looking a bit frantic. BJ was headed back in the direction of the farm—without Sophie. Barking furiously, he led Brian across several fields and right to Sophie. She had tried to maneuver through some fence wire like BJ did, but she couldn't quite pull it off and got stuck.

Our Jeep roared down the lane with only minutes to spare before we opened our gates. "Butch," Brian shouted, "I found her. You won't believe what she and BJ have been up to. I'll fill you in after we open. I'm putting her in her pen in the zoo. She's Okay, thank God."

The petting zoo played a role in all of Applewood Farm's public activities. We catered to families with young children, and the zoo was a favorite attraction. There were risks involved in having the public within touching distance of the animals. The safety of our customers was a major concern. Even with clear, cautionary signage, it was difficult to impress upon young parents how important it was to be vigilant while their children were around the animals.

When Sophie was a burro "teenager" and very affectionate, a lovely woman leaned over the petting zoo fence and scratched Sophie's head. Distracted, she did not notice that her little girl was attempting to crawl through the fence to give our pig Rocky, an apple. Luckily, Rocky did not mistake the child's fingers for apple. However, as the mother turned to care for her child, Sophie no longer felt she was getting the attention she deserved. She reached out teeth bared, and grabbed the top of the woman's breast in her teeth. Fortunately, the customer had a sense of humor and laughed it off.

School tours were a popular activity during pumpkin season. As the sun gradually ascended, the days warmed pleasantly without a trace of humidity. These were excellent conditions for 60 first graders and their parents to find the perfect pumpkin.

"Here come the buses, Butch! Are you ready in the barn?" Brian called from the parking area, just up the hill from the barn.

"Ready!" I shouted back. I just finished filling the big bin with crisp empire apples and poured cups of apple cider for a snack when the parents and children completed their tour.

Kids shot off the buses like kernels of corn spewing from an auger. Brian quickly organized the throng of 120. Parents arrived by car. He directed them to the hay wagons attached to the big, green John Deere tractor. All settled into place and off they went. First stop, the reindeer corral and an invitation to come visit our reindeer in December and find a Christmas tree.

The tour moved through fields of soybeans and feed corn. Farmer Brian kept everyone on the wagons while he gave a short educational talk on how pumpkins grow. Then, everyone scoured the pumpkin patch. Each child and parent got a small hold-in-both-hands-sized pumpkin to take home. That particular field was reserved exclusively for school tours.

Next, the children tumbled off the hay wagon like birds leaving the nest and the group hustled up to the barn to enjoy all the attractions inside and out. Squeals of delight pierced the morning air. Outside the barn, they spied the petting zoo, the kiddy maze, the playground, the pumpkin bowling game, and the model choo choo chugging around the big fir tree by the barn doors. Inside their snack waited and the model trains ran. A Halloween diorama displayed animated witches stirring their brew as Steiny, our cat, purred, preened and slept the day away. The Spooky Spot—a darkened room with one way in and out— featured not-too-scary vignettes ready to thrill the kids.

For the next thirty minutes, chaos ruled. Parents and children dashed and darted in and out, making sure not to miss anything. They moved like barn swallows chasing insects. Snacks distributed, I put on my cashier's hat and attended to the line that quickly formed at the checkout booth. Children practiced their math skills as they counted coins for their mementos. Parents paid for gourdes, corn shocks, mums, big pumpkins, gallons of apple cider, and pounds of apples.

Hearing that cash register ring warmed me to my toes. I reflected on how much I'd grown through the years with the retail end of our business. At first, I never touched the cash box to make change for customers having been a poor student when it came to math. My insecurities surfaced when handling money, fearful of making a mistake. The high school students I hired handled the job with aplomb, and that was fine with me. Over time, with coaching from Brian and telling myself I could manage it, I gained the confidence to tackle the chore myself, first with a cash box and eventually the cash register. This may seem a simple task, but to me, conquering it was huge.

Just as satisfying were the happy faces of children, parents and teachers as they ascended the small slope to board their buses. They looked delighted with their experience in Maryland agri-tourism. Applewood Farm was at the forefront of this new approach to keep agriculture alive and well. Other farmers throughout the state were beginning to follow suit, and it helped to make our farms more profitable as well as to introduce the public to local agriculture.

It's Only Money

My father kept a list of things ranked by importance. Money was at the top. Smart and shrewd, when it came to finances, he invested wisely in the stock market from an early age. He made a daily habit of studying the market's fluctuations and fickle nature. Mom, extremely good with figures, kept the books for him, but she didn't share Dad's consuming interest in the stock market. Dad often said that his primary goal was to "take care of his bride so she would never have to worry." He did just that. After he died, he left Mom financially secure … amply secure. We kids encouraged her to enjoy this new freedom, but she could never shed the weight of not living up to Dad's expectations. She continued to live frugally; the thought of spending "his" money left her feeling inadequate and insecure. She often lamented, "What if when I get to heaven, he makes me account for every penny I spent?"

"Mom, you'll be going to heaven, but what makes you so sure he'll be there?" I joked as we sat at her apartment dining table. "Dad's whole purpose was to leave you financially secure. I think you should enjoy it."

Even though we encouraged her to enjoy her inheritance, I understood what she meant. She was not going to relinquish habits honed over 60 years with a snap of her fingers. Twenty years after dad died, when Mom herself was under hospice care, she shared a troubled dream with us, her daughters, who were there for her in those final stages. As we gathered around, she spoke; propped up in the mechanical bed we placed near a sunny window in her bedroom.

"Last night I had a terrible dream about your father," Mom said. "There was a knocking at my apartment door. When I opened it there he stood, dressed in a black tuxedo and top hat. Can you imagine that?"

"No," we said in unison.

"He said, 'Em, how've you been spending my money?' I can't remember much of the rest," she said on the verge of tears. "I just know he's going to be waiting to take me to task." We tried everything to reassure her, to no avail.

Two days before she died, Mom's hospice nurse, a kind woman, strong and grounded, put Mom's mind at ease with a strategy to deal with Dad if and when she met him on the other side. I never learned the details of that plan, but we overheard a lot of guffawing and belly laughing as they strategized in the next room.

I, too, still dealt with demons from all those years ago, probably beginning with the time I saved up money for that used blue bike Dad wouldn't let me buy. Dad and Mom both thought my attitude toward money was too cavalier. In truth, as a single adult, I never missed paying a bill on time, I contributed regularly to a savings account, and I certainly never once asked my parents for money. I did foster their impression of me by intentionally irritating them when they challenged me about the necessity of a purchase I was making. "It's only money," I'd say, knowing full well the exasperation those words created. I made up my mind as a young adult that money would not consume me. It was a means to an end but not the primary goal.

In preparation for marriage, I made certain that all my bills were paid before walking down the aisle. Brian's financial approach was not the same. Applewood Farm challenged everything I knew and practiced regarding my—now our—finances. During the first 25 years on the farm, we were continually in debt, a fairly typical agricultural lifestyle.

Brian grew up rarely feeling the sting of denial except when he gave up chocolate during the 40 days of lent. Sacrifice was not in his lexicon unless it meant giving to others. The difference between our attitude toward paying bills, saving and gift giving is still apparent.

"Butch, should we send Jim and Cindy's son a check since he is graduating from medical school?" Brian asked me recently.

"We don't really know their son. At least I don't. You gave them two reindeer a few years back, remember? A nice card with a note should suffice, don't you think?" I said, knowing how this would turn out.

"I think it'd be nice if we include something for him in the card."

"Okay, whatever you think" I said, smiling to myself. In the past this would have been a real tug of war, because money was so tight. Brian still would have sent a generous check while I silently fumed.

For much of our marriage guilt plagued me for being a tightwad. Where I would send $50, Brian would send $100. Brian believed the finances would miraculously work out in the end. My faith needed propping up if I were to trust the same.

Brian's very spirit is magnanimous. He gives of his time, his treasure, his abundance of enthusiasm and positive outlook on life. I find it one of his most endearing and admirable qualities, but this very quality has been one of the hardest for me to accept. I've found it difficult being the one who says, "Let's think about this," or just a flat out, "No." I'd like to think I have a generous nature, but I truly pale in comparison to my husband. Brian's philosophy is that whatever you give comes back to you— sometime, some way—and usually in abundance. Time and again I have seen this proven over the years. That is not to say Brian hasn't been taken advantage of occasionally, but the scales definitely tilt in favor of the goodness of people. This insight and understanding increased my appreciation of my husband's philosophy.

In the last 15 years, my stranglehold on the family finances eased. After Brian began working full time on the farm and we started growing pumpkins, conducting school tours, hosting parties, and holding reindeer educational programs, the farm began holding its own. We worked our way into the black on the balance sheet. Thankfully, we managed to have civil conversations on the sensitive subject of the almighty dollar—tense but respectful. I came to recognize that I expertly tamped down my frustrated feelings. No doubt this was a contributor to my bouts with depression. Professional counseling helped me acknowledge this tendency and develop a healthier approach.

After Mom died in July 2001 and we settled her estate, we siblings each received a sizeable inheritance, thanks to Dad's planning and Mom's reluctance to squander any of the nest egg. Brian and I chose to pay off all our debts: the mortgage on the farm, the operating and equipment loans, and a car loan. The financial cloud that hovered evaporated, but I found myself enveloped by a deepening melancholy.

Road Trip

"Road Trip!" Brian enthused. We drove out the farm lane. Spring rain pelted the windshield. The year was 2003. Our destination: a meeting of the Reindeer Owners and Breeders Association in Pendleton, Oregon.

"We should be out of this glop by the time we reach Western Maryland, Butch," Brian reassured me. I hunkered down in my seat in our white Volkswagen Passat. A map spread across my legs so I could help with the navigation, my mood as gray as the sky. Brian hoped the cross-country trip would raise my spirits, bringing me back to the fun-loving Butch he knew. I wanted the distraction of sightseeing to quiet the negative voices reluctant to give me release.

On top of Mom's death, my favorite uncle died the following April. I tried to free myself from the depression that turned my world dark and colorless; somewhere inside hid the old me: positive, decisive, energetic, enthusiastic, enjoying life's challenges. But now everything seemed a struggle.

"Butch, do you want to go out to dinner tonight?" Brian might ask.

"I don't care. You decide," I often said. This represented a typical exchange. Berating myself, I feared I'd exhaust Brian's patience. Rita, the psychiatrist I saw weekly, encouraged me. "Pat, I've never seen anyone work as hard as you do to try to fix yourself," she observed one afternoon. "You need to let yourself process what we discuss here and not expect instant results. Grief wends its own way. It can't be hurried, pushed, or shoved."

I did expect results. I understood I was grieving. Intellectually, looking at all aspects of those relationships. It didn't seem to make any difference. When Mom was diagnosed with terminal cancer, it was the right time to retire from my APG personnel position. Home from Oregon after caring for Mom during her last six weeks, I'd been fine and dealing well since she died. Her care was, for me, an unexpected gift of shared joys, memories, and heartaches. Grief and tears swept over me like rough waves as we tended to Mom in her final days.

Back at Applewood farm, I threw myself into preparations for the pumpkin season. Impressed by the hospice workers who tended to Mom, I even joined a local hospice chapter as a volunteer. I thought I had done all my grieving in Oregon, and the hospice administrator agreed, "Pat we don't generally accept anyone into our training program until at least a year after the death of someone close," she said. "However, you seem to be adjusting just fine so let's give it a try and see how it goes." I recruited a friend to join me for the training.

Once a week for six weeks we traveled the 50 minutes into Towson to learn the ins and outs of caring for those in the last stages of life. Afterwards, my assignments included several dear folks. But when the winter of 2003 hit, the farm quieted, the days shortened into darkness, and my spirits and mood gradually slipped. I listened closely as my inner voice seemed to say, "You're not ready for this." My work with the dying, while rewarding, propelled me toward a vortex of despair.

Hunkered under the weight of this octopus perched on my shoulder, its tentacles wrapped me in a suffocating hold. What was I really grieving? Desperate for answers and afraid, I deferred to Brian for almost everything. My hospice volunteering stopped. I managed to get out of bed, keep up with laundry and cook meals … any routines that didn't require me to think or make decisions. God would surely help this malaise to pass quickly. My doctor prescribed anti-depressants to no effect. Angry, impatient, and not easy to live with, I dreaded that Brian's patience would run out—and so might he.

Stalwart and true, Brian hung in there. Now, we were on this trip toward Pendleton, planning to see the northern United States and visit relatives along the way. We reached the Maryland—Pennsylvania border, and the rain eased. As each mile clicked by, my dark cloud lightened. There's something about driving west and crossing the great Mississippi River that feeds my soul. Traffic lightens, people dress casually, life's pace measurably slows, and shopkeepers take time to share local lore. Such a contrast to the busyness of the East.

At the conclusion of our reindeer meeting, we met up with my sister Maureen, who planned to drive to the far eastern corner of the state to explore a little-known town called Joseph. She had read an article in *The Oregonian* about the town revitalizing its main street with bronzes from its local foundries, and she asked if we would join her to take a look. We agreed. As the Wallowa Mountains came into view, I exclaimed, "Look Reen, it's just like Switzerland!" We both skied in the Swiss Alps as young adults. The vista that stretched before us reawakened those carefree days. My spirits soared with the hawks and eagles against an azure sky. The tentacles of grief loosened further.

We checked into the Bronze Antler B & B, welcomed by Heather and Bill, who recently retired from Army careers to settle in this rustic and charming corner of the west. Over a bountiful breakfast, Heather sat with us and shared her extensive knowledge of Joseph and the surrounding Eaglecap Wilderness. Under her tutelage we were well equipped for our exploration of the town and surrounding area.

Brian took off to check out the lake and trails. Maureen and I walked a few blocks into town to scope out the beautiful bronze sculptures along Joseph's cobblestoned sidewalks and to visit the unique shops. There was not a stoplight in the entire county, the size of which was bigger than the whole state of Maryland.

The county had 7,000 inhabitants (1,000 of them in Joseph), and the dog population probably doubled that. Not just any kind of dog, these dogs worked for a living and traveled everywhere with their owners on the backs of "rigs," Wallowa County speak for "pickup truck." We watched the dog action with amusement wherever we went. Every rig had at least two, usually three, border collies chasing each other around the truck bed while traveling at 60 miles an hour down the road. When parked, the dogs strutted and snapped with attitude, protecting their turf from the dogs on a neighboring rig as their owner-ranchers shopped for supplies in town. When not engaged in protective duties, they lulled peacefully, totally at rest except for their watchful and intelligent eyes.

We met Brian for a hearty lunch at the Mountainier Café. We sat spellbound as we gazed through the picture windows at the Wallowa Mountains still cloaked in snow in mid-June. Peaks sparkled in the midday sun. We topped off our meal with the Café's famous triple berry cobbler that did not disappoint.

After the third day of our stay in Joseph, Brian and I headed north to Glacier National Park, and Maureen turned west toward home in Hood River.

"Butch, what'd you think of Joseph?" Brian asked as we drove toward Lewiston, Idaho.

"It's a whole lot more than I expected. I kind 'a feel like I left a little piece of myself there this morning. What about you?"

"You know, when we drove down that grade three days ago—someone told me it's called the Minam Grade—and I was stopping at every turn to take pictures. I've never seen country like this before. When we came into Enterprise and Joseph and those mountains—well, they're unbelievably beautiful." Brian sounded as wistful as I felt.

"What was the best part?" I asked.

"While you and Reen explored all the shops and galleries in town, I drove up into the hills, around that sapphire blue lake … I wanted to go into that wilderness and ride slopes on horseback. But, you know, most of all? The people. The contrast between east and west is crystal clear in Joseph. Everyone, without exception, took time to answer questions. They seemed interested and anxious that visitors appreciate their town as much as they do."

"You know what Reen and I found amazing?" I interjected. "While we were strolling the street and came to a crosswalk, traffic actually stopped, yielding us the right of way. We saw locals chatting in the middle of the street and trucks and cars waiting patiently as they took their time clearing the way. I agree with you about how friendly and helpful everyone seemed. I'm really glad Reen suggested this. For all the years I lived in Oregon, I never knew about Joseph."

"How come?" Brian glanced at me.

"I think that once Dad and Mom drove us west to Hood River in 1945, they had little interest in exploring the eastern part of the state. When I was in my early teens Mom did take the four of us to a dude ranch outside of Pendleton for a week in August."

"Did your Dad go too?" asked Brian.

"No, as I remember he was harvesting pears. I'm sure we had more fun without him, and Mom was relaxed. Pete was only about five years old. It was a fun week but very hot, dry, dusty, and desert-like. I've never liked that kind of topography. But Joseph, in contrast, is all lush green and jutting mountains" I said.

We drove on, picnicking beside the Clearwater River enroute to Glacier National Park, which wasn't on our original itinerary. Folks we met along the way during our trip encouraged us to include it. Because it was late June, we were assured that the roads would be clear and open. Wildlife sightings would be frequent. We were told that the Going-to-the-Sun Road, which connects the west and east sectors of the park, was not to be missed. After a day of driving through magnificent, winding canyons and along clear-flowing rivers, we arrived at Flat Head Lake in the southwest corner of the park. The next morning, we began a scenic, hair-raising 52-mile trek on the two-lane road to the sun, crossing the Continental Divide at 7,000 feet through snow-patched Logan Pass.

"Brian, look. Look! Here out my window! A big horn sheep!" The narrow lane was so curvy that Brian had to keep his eyes glued to the road. But at that moment traffic came to a standstill.

"Oh, man isn't he beautiful and regal. He's coming closer, Butch. I bet if you put the window down he'd stick his head in."

"He acts like he owns the road, doesn't he? Well, he kind a does right now." I said in amazement as this wild animal sauntered down the road, then stepped off the shear edge into thin air and disappeared.

We stayed in the picturesque Lodge at St Mary's, where every view filled our senses with beauty. Their restaurant offered delicious meals of buffalo and elk steak. A Park Service boat trip around Lake McDonald educated us on geological wonders in the area. One sunny morning, we took a trail ride on quiet steeds that allowed us to inhale crisp, pristine air, while taking in views of alpine meadows and interesting wildlife. A hike around Swiftcurrent Lake in the Many Glacier Region of the park coupled with a visit to a splendid historic lodge built in the early part of the 20th century filled one of our days. Over dinner on our final evening we reflected on our adventures and the highlights of our trip. The next morning, I thought regretfully, we would point east.

"Butch, it's time to go—you've got to get up," Brian urged. I burrowed deeper into the warm covers. "Come on we're heading home today. Let's get a move on."

"I don't want to," I mumbled. Like a fine, penetrating mist, that dark melancholy fog slithered over me. It twisted and grasped, tugging me back into the lonely muddle. Why didn't the thought of home to Maryland, to the farm, quicken my heart? Brian's excitement to start back across the country was palpable but not contagious.

"Come on, Butch. We need to see our herd. You know they're missing us. Steiny is going to be so glad to see you. She'll crawl right into your lap and purr her heart out. Get up. I'll meet you in the dining room for breakfast in 30 minutes." Concern etched Brian's face as he left.

With the car packed, we began: I with my foot on an imaginary brake, and Brian with his heart on the accelerator. Miles clicked away, and the dread weighing me down intensified.

As our trip came to an end and we rolled down the farm lane, I sighed wishing I felt more enthusiastic about returning to this place I loved.

It took three more months for me to work through the grief and depression. Mowing between the Christmas trees was a job that was predictable and necessary. Hours of solitude on the Dixie Chopper, our zero-radius mower, must have helped ease the grief or allowed me to numb myself in thoughtlessness.

On a clear late-September mornings in the barn, cleaning and preparing for the pumpkin season, I felt a niggle and stopped. I looked around with wonder and excitement and then realized *I'm back!*

A Piece of Oregon

That December, I made plans to fly west to attend a trade show in Seattle to resupply the farm gift shop. I told Brian I planned to pick up Maureen on the way.

"Well, you know, Butch, I think I'll fly out with you and go back to Joseph."

"Are you kidding? Not without me you're not." I had gotten a whiff of adventure. Since concluding our road trip in June, we'd precious little time to talk much about Joseph. Now the dam had been breached. In our typical full-steam-ahead mode, I made travel arrangements. Impulsively, Brian emailed a real estate agent to show us some properties at that beautiful Wallowa Lake.

Prior to my planned buying trip to Seattle with Maureen we flew to Boise, Idaho, rented a 4-wheel drive SUV and headed west toward Wallowa County and Joseph. As the Wallowa Mountains came into view, we shared a knowing look of excitement. The peaks wore their full winter coat. Deep snow was everywhere. We settled into our rental and hustled over to the real estate office to announce our arrival.

A woman named Judy Willis greeted us warmly. "Welcome to Joseph. This must be different from your weather in Maryland. You're really seeing what winter is like here!"

"It looks beautiful. The mountains are amazing. The contrast between June and January is dramatic," Brian said.

"I know you mentioned in your email that you're interested in properties at the lake," said Judy, "but right now I only have one property up there. It might be tough getting to it because of road conditions."

Undaunted, Brian pressed, "I have four-wheel drive, if that'd help."

"Well, I do too. That's not the issue," Judy demurred. "The county doesn't maintain side roads at the lake, but we can give it a try. How about you meet me here at 9 tomorrow?"

We spent that night cuddled in front of the fire, discussing and reminiscing. When Mom died, we four children needed to decide what to do with the orchard. Each of us knew Dad felt strongly that we should never sell. Maureen and I wanted to keep it in the family and I, being married to a farmer, thought Brian and I could manage it. To do that we needed to buy out my brother and two sisters. I proposed that my share of Mom's estate go toward their payment. However, Ellen and Pete thought we'd get more for the orchard by selling. Taking our father's edict and my emotional attachment out of the equation, the path to follow was clear.

We sold the orchard to the Davis boys, neighbor orchardists for 45 years. Twenty-five years earlier, Dad negotiated a lease agreement with the Davis boys and approved their horticultural practices. Since the orchard had to be sold, I took consolation in the fact that Dad had handpicked them as new stewards of his land. As a result, Brian and I were now in Oregon with a chunk of money.

The prospect of owning a piece of Oregon land made me almost dizzy. I squelched the thought 30 years before when I realized Brian was unlikely to leave his home state and family. The roots we sunk on Applewood Farm were deep for us both, and I gave little thought to living elsewhere. But Brian promoted the idea of life in the Wallowas. For our whole married lives, a great distance had separated me from my family. More importantly, while at the farm, we never relaxed. We worked one way or another all the time. On the rare occasions we left the farm, the constant brain chatter stopped and we wound down like tops.

Judy drove us up Main Street toward the lake, and she chatted away. The sapphire blue lake of summer lay white and pristine, ringed by a necklace of stately evergreens flocked in snow. Approaching the head of the lake was like entering an enchanted, frozen forest. We hopped from the car into deep snow, crusted with a layer of ice.

"The property is down this slope," said Judy. "We're going to have to be really careful we don't lose footing and slide right down to the main road!" I stepped gingerly, testing my footing. I felt like a raggedy Dorothy Hamill on ice skates.

"We'd better not hang on to each other," said Brian. "You and Judy aim for that pipe fence that leads down to the cabin and dig your heels in to break the crust."

We stomped the surface like storm troopers, giggling nervously as we tried to gain purchase. It took a minute to catch our breath.

"Judy, you're right," I said. A cloud of frozen breath puffed in front of me. I studied the lay of the land. "This icy crust is so hard, but it looks like a billowy marshmallow." I laughed and felt a welling of happiness at the possibilities ahead.

"Pat, remember, this cabin has only been used as a summer getaway," she said. "Also, as a hunting retreat by the doctor's family. It's rustic to be sure."

Judy pulled back a screened door adorned with whimsical skunks. We stepped inside a large knotty-pine great room with picture windows extending its full length and a stone fireplace at the far end. I stood bewildered. It felt just like our home at the orchard, but with more light. I made my way through the accumulated furniture and knickknacks. It seemed colder inside than out, but Judy explained the cabin had been winterized at the end of the summer season. All the pipes were drained, and the heat was turned off. We continued to explore and found three good-sized bedrooms with closets. Our farmhouse had few closets. The cabin needed work, especially in the two bathrooms, but it had potential. I re-entered the main room and caught Brian's eye. We exchanged knowing smiles.

"Judy, I think we've seen enough," said Brian through chattering teeth. "We'd better try and make it back up that hill to your SUV before we freeze to death. Maybe you can tell us more once we warm up."

As we settled into Judy's vehicle with the heater going full blast, she said, "As I mentioned, this cabin is currently owned by a doctor's family in Walla Walla who used it as a vacation retreat. The father died, and none of his eight boys wanted—or were in a position—to keep the cabin in the family. They're only the second owners. The first was a lumber baron out of La Grande who built it in the 1930s for his family to enjoy. Through those trees there," she pointed, "you can see the lake, but it's hard today because of all the snow."

"Judy, what about all the stuff: pine furniture, books, dishes, beds, lamps, linens?" I asked.

"It all goes with the sale. I think the original owner built all that pine cabinetry and the current owners just kept it."

Later in the evening over drinks, Brian and I discussed whether it made sense for us to make an offer on the cabin. "Are you serious about owning property in Oregon, Brian?" I asked.

"I'm sure—I love it here, and I think that cabin has personality. You know, Butch, Judy mentioned the lake area is a popular summer resort. We might talk to her about putting the cabin on the rental market during the season. That way any improvements we make would be a business expense, including our travel to and from Oregon."

"Well, I like that for sure," I said.

A second look convinced us we should make an offer. We determined that the cabin had good bones. To get it ready for the rental season by Memorial Day, we'd fly out in late April and initially do cosmetic enhancements. Later, we might consider a kitchen and bath renovation. At Judy's suggestion, we met with Cindi Ashenbrenner to arrange rental management of the cabin. Cindi seemed as excited as we were at the prospect of including our cabin on her list of properties. Another piece of the puzzle fell cleanly into place.

On March 31, 2004, we became the proud owners of the hunter green log cabin trimmed in barn red on Forest Dell Road in Joseph, Oregon. The first day of May found us hard at work at the cabin sorting, tossing, cleaning, fixing. There were hundreds of books lining shelves, stacked on the floor, stored in boxes. My weakness for books almost jeopardized the whole operation. I caressed each book, thought about its previous owner, and decided which to keep. Books tell a lot about a person: their interests, sports, and philosophy. I felt a connection to Mrs. McClellan, the doctor's wife and previous owner, and hoped one day we would meet.

With two weeks to accomplish our task, we used our rental agent's inventory list to comfortably outfit the cabin for the summer season. Brian took care of plumbing, electrical and any structural fixes, while I attempted to make the interior welcoming and attractive.

Inspired by the green siding and red roof of the cabin, it facilitated carrying those colors throughout the interior. Before our May spruce-up session, I had scrambled to order supplies like flatware, sheets, and blankets. Having a theme gave me a structure and most things fell neatly into place. We relied on help and suggestions from local craftsmen, professionals, neighbors, shopkeepers, ranchers, and farmers to accomplish the job in the time allotted. We received a very warm welcome and many acquaintances grew to become friends. We sensed that folks in Wallowa County possessed open-mindedness and tolerance, which was a foretelling of the years to come.

The challenge of decorating this diamond in the rough with a little of this and that, old and new, revved my resourceful juices into overdrive. The only large store of any kind, somewhat close to Joseph was Walmart, an hour and a half away in La Grande, weather permitting. Big box stores like Costco or Home Depot were two and a half hours in the opposite direction: out the North Highway, up and down Snow Hollow, Buford, Rattlesnake, and Asotin Grades, a harrowing, unforgettable drive

222

for newcomers even in good weather. This route took Maureen and I to Clarkson, Washington, or across the Snake River to Lewiston, Idaho—veritable shopping meccas by western standards. The scenery captured my breath and held it through twisty, rock-strewn, hairpin turns with few guardrails that kept a vehicle from plunging thousands of feet to the canyon floor. This disregard for protective rails terrified me, as it delivered me breathless and panting to the bottom of Asotin Grade.

The real eye-opener occurred one May afternoon when Brian and I headed to the Walmart in La Grande. Rain pelted our rental truck's windshield as we approached the store. Fortunately, Brian thought to bring tarps and ropes to keep everything dry and secure. Armed with long lists for every room in the cabin, we each took a shopping cart.

Four hours and $4,000 later, quite frazzled, I trudged through the rain to the truck. It was almost hidden under a mountain of Walmart goods, neatly and expertly packed by Brian. We came close to entirely furnishing every room of the cabin.

As the two weeks of frantic work wound to a close, we looked around at the cabin's transformation with a sense of pride. We invited Judy to come take a look. "My word, you guys, it doesn't even look like the same cabin. Now it's so warm and cozy—I'm sure it'll be really successful during the rental season."

"Judy, we hate to leave but we've got to get back to the farm. So we'll be heading for Boise tomorrow morning and fly out for Maryland the next day," Brian explained.

"Thanks for all your help and support, Judy," I said, giving her a farewell hug.

Hidden Treasure

A myriad of emotions were reflected on Bryce's usually jovial face, I saw fear, doubt, anxiety, shame, sadness, and courage, to name a few. My stomach was in knots as I watched him struggle to get the words out—the reason for this unexpected visit.

"Mom, Dad, my life is never going to be the same" he said quietly.

"Well, that sounds serious. What do you mean?" asked Brian.

"Katie is pregnant, and I'm the father," Bryce announced, eyes downcast.

Bryce had met Katie several months before at Looney's Pub in Bel Air, where he had come close to getting into a fight with Jeff, the father of Katie's four-year-old daughter. Bryce claimed that Jeff had become ignorant with Katie and wouldn't leave her alone. Bryce stepped in and convinced Jeff to buzz off. We had met Katie and her daughter Lisi once, when I had invited them for Christmas dinner.

We knew little about Katie because Bryce was very closed-mouthed about her. Over Christmas dinner we learned that she and Lisi lived with her parents about 2 miles away from the farm and she worked at a Bel Air car dealership. She was 24 years old, with long black hair, big dark eyes, and lovely milk-white skin. She was petite, intelligent and gorgeous. She never married Lisi's father, although Katie claimed they tried to make a go of it. Katie explained that Jeff had issues with alcohol and drugs, and she didn't want her daughter exposed to that.

On this fateful evening in mid-February 2005, Bryce was 25 years old and employed by a local trucker, as well as working on our farm during open seasons.

"Oh my!" I gasped "Well I guess you're right about this changing your life. When is Katie due?"

"Late August or early September. I want you to know Katie and I are soul mates. I've never felt about anyone like I feel about her," Bryce asserted.

"So, what're your intentions?" Brian asked.

"We plan to rent a house and move in together for now. I've a friend who has a place in Rock Springs and he'd really like us to take it."

"Bryce, this really does come as a shock. But Mom and I want you to know we will support you and Katie in whatever you decide. However, I'd like you to consider an alternative: you rent the house, pay all the bills, but don't move in until you two decide if you're going to marry. That way you'll both have some breathing space to sort things out."

"Dad, I can't do that. Katie already has a daughter, and I won't leave them alone to fend for themselves. We're not going to get married now, but wait and see how things work out."

What did work out was that Bryce and Katie welcomed the most amazing son on September 6, 2005, and named him Mason Bryce Adelhardt. There is no doubt in our minds that Katie is a caring and loving mother, and she certainly made childbirth look easy. I know this because she invited me in to witness Mason's arrival, and I will always treasure that experience.

Sadly, Bryce and Katie could not find common ground to solidify their relationship, but over the years they have developed a working friendship that serves to benefit Mason. Now, at 10 years old, Mason has grown into a well rounded, smart, gregarious, funny, and interesting young man. He can discuss almost any subject, which makes for interesting conversations on politics and world affairs. Time spent with him is fun, and we look forward to his arrival in Oregon each July to spend one-on-one time with us and attend the Chief Joseph Day Camp.

We will always be grateful for Mason's presence in our lives. He has enriched us beyond measure and brings continuous joy as we watch him grow into a young man.

Letting Go

Each April promised a trip west to prepare our cabin for the rental season. Returning again in late August to escape Maryland's heat and humidity and to revel in the cool mountain air of Joseph. It was an adventure becoming acquainted with this bustling little town and everyone in it. We discovered that folks were less twisted up in traditions and inhibitions than in the east. Most days, included a hike on one of the many trails or a drive. It was a revelation to learn never to depart on an exploratory trip without a full tank of gas. Coming from the congested east, it amazed us that we could drive for two or three hours and not meet a single vehicle or settlement. The landscape and roads were rugged, rough, and remote. The beauty and peace enveloped us. Each visit felt like it ended prematurely leaving us wanting more, but duty called. Applewood Farm, and particularly the animals, depended on us. Letting go of what we worked so hard to create—I couldn't imagine it. I felt like my very identity was a projection of Applewood Farm. I hoped I'd recognize when the time was right to retire from farm work.

Bryce graduated in 2002 with a degree in Agri-Business from Delaware Valley College and returned home. During the next three years he worked various jobs and helped us on the farm during open season. While Bryce claimed he loved the farm, it didn't seem he was prepared to engage in our agri-tourism business. Our goal was to avoid the pitfalls of children taking over a family business. Without forcing the issue, we hoped that Bryce would want to take over the reins.

By 2006, Applewood Farm begged to leap to the next level, but Brian and I didn't have the energy to take it there. The prudent thing to do was close the business after our pumpkin and Christmas seasons that year. Bryce agreed. I looked forward to starting a new chapter in our farm life.

One evening, Bryce joined us for dinner and we took the opportunity to outline our plans for 2007. Brian began, "When Mom starts the marketing for this upcoming Christmas season, we'll announce that it'll be our final year. We've decided to continue the pumpkin operation since the fall is such a nice time of year."

I interjected, "We still like doing pumpkins. Christmas—it gets so cold and we think we're getting too old to keep doing it. But, Bryce, if you want to keep planting trees and manage that profit center, we'll fully support you."

Bryce shuffled in his chair; his foot tapped nervously "No, Mom. I don't want to disappoint you, but I don't like the Christmas tree operation. It's too much handwork. With pumpkins and the corn maze you can do everything with machines—that I like."

"You're not disappointing us," Brian said. "Mom and I both want you to do what'll make you happy."

We had an exceptional Christmas season partly due to our announcement that it was Applewood Farm's final holiday season. Customers flocked in droves, seeking Brian or me.

"We're so disappointed to hear you won't have a Christmas season anymore," some said.

"We've been bringing our family here since our kids were little. Now they're bringing their kids. It's terrible there won't be a place like this to create wonderful memories," others said.

The crescendo of voices increased like the Halleluiah Chorus. We told our customers that if they really felt that way, they should talk to Bryce.

At the conclusion of our second weekend in December we sat at the kitchen table, and Bryce said, "Mom, Dad, as I picked up trees these last two weekends, everyone urged me to keep our Christmas tree season going."

"Bryce, we've heard the same," I said.

"What're you thinking?" Brian asked.

"Well, I'm not sure. I never realized how much what we do here means to people."

"Whatever you decide, we'll support your decision," Brian said reassuringly.

By the end of our season, Bryce received so much positive reinforcement from customers that he decided to continue the Christmas operation. Even the newspapers joined the drumbeat and printed celebratory articles about the son at Applewood Farm "continuing the legacy."

I hoped this meant that Bryce would truly engage and want to be involved in all aspects of our operation. For the 2008 open season we decided to restructure, giving each of us a profit center to manage. Our intention was to allow each of us some separate independence. By my observation, we were winding down and letting Bryce take hold. However, after our selling season, we sat down to assess the year and make plans for 2009, we realized our division of labor had not worked.

Although, Bryce told us his trucking boss had been in full agreement with giving him time to devote to the family farm, Bryce offered excuses, prioritizing his truck-driving job. We were left to pick up the slack. This in spite of including Bryce in our plans and discussions the previous January so all options and expectations were out in the open. Our intention was to include him in every stage of our yearly cycle. In review, we determined that 2008 proved one of our very best and our worst years. The best, due to record turnouts; the worst, due to sick reindeer and Brian's aging parents. Coupled with Brian battling Lyme's disease and Bryce's continued reluctance to fully assume his duties, these hardships made for more than I could bear.

One warm September day in 2008 I worked in the barn on gift shop displays. I tried hanging a large, unwieldy pedal tractor for display. It was too cumbersome and heavy for me to do alone. I interrupted Brian's wagon repairs to see if he could help me. As he entered the barn, I knew from the look on his face that his repairs were not going well.

"What do you need, Butch?" Brian asked.

"I'm sorry if I caught you at a bad time. I thought this pedal tractor would display nicely if we hung it from the ceiling over here." I pointed, indicating how I envisioned it.

"Does it have to be done right now?" he said, exasperation evident in his look and stance.

"Well, I guess it can wait, or I can figure out something else." Brian was tired, as was I. He looked like he could chew nails.

"Butch, the truth is, I think it's a good idea, but I'm so sick of doing stuff for this gift shop—you know ... it just isn't fun anymore. None of it's fun anymore."

"I've been thinking the exact same thing, Brian. I don't have the energy anymore to make our great ideas come to fruition. The farm needs younger and smarter minds. People with fire in their bellies." I listened to what we were saying and knew the time had come for us to stop.

Decisively Brian agreed, "After this pumpkin and Christmas season, let's call it quits. We'll talk with Bryce and give him a deadline to let us know if he really does want to take over and continue. Like, February 1st. What do you think, Butch?"

"That's probably a good idea. It's time, but I'm convinced Bryce is unsure. Maybe he's afraid of not living up to our expectations."

Brian wrinkled his brow and nodded.

"His actions and lack of enthusiasm seem to indicate that he's not interested. I want to think for a while about how we should approach Bryce," I was relieved that we reached a decision but somewhat anxious about working out the details of a transition.

Previously, in the fall of 2008, Harford County approached us about selling the farm's development rights. This statewide plan enabled farmers to receive payment for their acreage if they agreed to never sell their land for development. The county had been after us to sell for eight years. Now, maybe the time was right to take advantage of this offer. Financially, this would allow us the freedom to actually retire to the beckoning of our cozy cabin in Joseph, Oregon. If we stayed on the farm, it would be hard to let go of the business we had nursed for over 35 years. If we moved off the farm it would give Bryce the freedom to develop and introduce his own methods without us peering over his shoulder.

It was a cold day toward the end of January when Bryce called. "Mom, can you and Dad meet me for lunch at Delta Pizza tomorrow?"

"Yes, Bryce, I think that'll work. What's on your mind?"

"I want to talk to you guys about the farm."

"Okay, that's great. What time?" I asked, my heart beating like a snare drum, secretly hoping Bryce's decision would be to not continue public seasons at the farm. It wasn't his dream. We wanted him to find what gave him the same pleasure and joy we had found working the farm.

We settled in and ordered. Bryce didn't waste any time coming to the point. "I've decided I want to continue with pumpkins and the Christmas tree sales."

"Wow! Okay, Bryce. You're sure? Because if you just want to grow crops or even rent out the ground, we're fine with that too," Brian said. "Mom and I've also made a decision."

"What's that?" asked Bryce.

"We're going to move to our cabin in Oregon in June. We don't want you to think we're abandoning you, but we really think it'd be easier for you if we weren't breathing down your neck."

"And Bryce," I added, "Dad and I have made a commitment to clean out the farmhouse so it'll be available for you to move into. We've agreed that we won't leave until the attic, basement, and every cupboard and closet have been cleaned out. It'll still be fully furnished and equipped, but we want you to consider it yours."

"I don't feel like you're abandoning me. I don't know if I'll be moving to the farm right away. I kind of like my set up at the Rose's farm right now."

"Bryce do you think it'd help if I prepared a list of things to do monthly?" I asked.

"Well, Mom, if you want to go to the trouble. But I think I pretty well know what you do," Bryce responded confidently.

My exasperation was simmering, so I couched my words: "Bryce, since you've never worked with or in any of my profit centers, it'd make me feel better if I at least left you a timeline that you can refer to." I felt like a deflated balloon and also incensed that Bryce assumed he understood everything that I'd done and could just pick up when we left. My heart hurt with this reality. Once the annual timeline was completed for Bryce, I would let go.

Sitting in my car overlooking the farm at the top of Applewood's lane after lunch that day, my head dropped to the steering wheel as tears of anger and frustration ran down my cheeks. As the tears dried and composure was regained, I understood the transition wouldn't be seamless. It was the right thing to do, for us and for Bryce. While there was a sense of sadness in the realization we would be leaving the dream we'd worked hard to create, I looked forward with anticipation to life in the West.

As promised, in May 2010 we headed west. As I write this, we have completed our fifth year in our comfy cabin in the mountains and Bryce's fifth year managing the farm. He calls when he needs help, but for the most part he has singlehandedly succeeded. He has also moved into the old farmhouse. Bryce has done many things differently than we would have, but with each passing year his engagement with Applewood grows and deepens.

In November 2014, we returned to the farm to help Bryce through the holiday season, as we have done each year since 2010. However, this time the experience and we were different. Instead of telling Bryce what we thought should be done, we asked what he wanted us to do and then we did it—his way. Our change in attitude produced immediate, positive results. They were heartwarmingly apparent in our interactions with Bryce. I've released my stranglehold and am at peace.

The personal growth I have realized since moving into the welcoming environment of Joseph has been unprecedented. I've shed crippling inhibitions that constrained me in the past and like a flower planted in rich soil, I've grown. I've spent time really listening but also freely sharing. Treasured friendships have resulted. It is liberating to find my place and fit in. I know I now own the life skills required to facilitate such a transition. I am confident I can employ them wherever I am.

Here in Joseph, Oregon, the five-mile drive to town that I'm privileged to make most days from our cabin still moves me. The sight of the Wallowa Mountains on a clear, brilliant day inspires and pulls at my heart. On an overcast day, whatever the clouds do—wispy or bold, white or threatening, like a symphony in that big sky—fills me with awe. These mountains speak to me of stability, strength, and beauty and they fill my soul.

As time goes on there will be change. The impact of the mountains I love so much is possible because of their peaks and valleys. Likewise, life will continue to offer the same, but on my life journey I recognize the need for, and fought hard to gain, self-awareness and healing. Those two hard earned gifts will live inside me no matter where my travels take me.

Acknowledgements

Wallowa County, Oregon is home to Fishtrap a writers organization promoting "good writing, in and about the West." It was through Fishtrap I was fortunate to take advantage of its many offerings and where this memoir began. Katey Schultz, an itinerate and talented intern, offered a three week memoir writing class. It proved so successful and rewarding participants convinced Fishtrap to allow Katey to add on another three weeks. When it came to molding my writing into something interesting Katey had a huge task before her. My experience was limited to government memos that tended to be long and dull. At the conclusion of our six weeks, Katey agreed to take three of us on as long distance, digital students. Thus Idella Allen, Amy Zahm and I worked with Katey for 3-plus years. Katey has published *Flashes of War*, continues to teach and been the recipient of many literary awards.

Simultaneously, I was invited to join a local writer's group, the Write Women, who gave me a safe place to read what I'd written offering thoughtful critiques, love, tears and laughter. I am forever grateful for their company and sharing of their own amazing writing and stories: Idella Allen, Leita Barlow, Annette Byrd, Cathy Putnum, Maxine Stone, Katherine Strickroth, Evelyn Swart, Janie Tippett, Lynn Uchinson, Ruth Wineteer, and Amy Zahm.

To Brian, my loving husband, who throughout this past decade has been unflaggingly supportive. To others who read and offered helpful critiques and encouragement: Jess and Steve Healey, Nick Acocella, Ginny Roeloffs, Maureen Higgins, Angie Rubin, Becky Klingler, Amy Zahm.

Gratitude and appreciation to Debbie Jennings whose boundless creativity, thoughtful insights and critiques were instrumental in keeping this project moving toward a conclusion.